l education for special needs

Physical Education for Special Needs

EDITED BY LILIAN GROVES

CAMBRIDGE UNIVERSITY PRESS
Cambridge
London · New York · Melbourne

To the PEA

Published by the Syndics of the Cambridge University Press
The Pitt Building, Trumpington Street, Cambridge CB2 1RP
Bentley House, 200 Euston Road, London NW1 2DB
32 East 57th Street, New York, NY 10022, USA
296 Beaconsfield Parade, Middle Park, Melbourne 3206, Australia

First published 1979

Printed in Great Britain
at the University Press, Cambridge

Library of Congress Cataloguing in Publication Data

Main entry under title:

Physical education for special needs.

Bibliography: p.

Includes index.

1. Physical education for handicapped children.
I. Groves, Lilian, 1928–
GV445.P5 371.9′044 78-68389
ISBN 0 521 22391 1
ISBN 0 521 29471 1 pbk

Contents

Introduction

Some years ago the Physical Education Association of Great Britain and Northern Ireland held a conference on 'Physical education for exceptional children'. The response was tremendous and made clear the need for greater dissemination of information about physical education and sport for children who are handicapped. Since that time there has been a great increase in the number of agencies concerned with this work and the names and addresses of some of the more important ones are included in the appendix of this book. Meanwhile, the PEA has continued to run annual conferences which are enthusiastically supported by physical educationalists, physiotherapists and teachers working in special schools seeking to increase their expertise. It is clear that few college physical education courses take note of work with handicapped children and most special education diploma courses make no mention of physical education.

Most of those contributing to this book have attempted to fill this gap by lecturing, demonstrating and writing articles. There seemed, in addition, a clear need for a publication which would offer practical suggestions but which would also lead teachers to develop their own ideas.

There is an obvious danger that in trying to cover a wide variety of handicaps (and most people agree that handicaps seldom come singly) such a publication as this might be too superficial to be of value to anyone. The problem in selecting areas to be covered in the end was less one of what should be included than of what should be left out.

There is no attempt here to look in detail at types of handicap; it is essential that teachers discuss individual children with the school medical officer. The medical information included in certain chapters is intended to help those not yet involved at first hand with these particular handicaps. In any event there is a danger of generalising about disabilities and suggesting that the same programme is appropriate for all children in the same category.

The emphasis in this book is on ability rather than disability and on enjoyable activity rather than therapeutic manipulation. Inevitably the areas chosen reflect the interests of the editor. Some readers may be disappointed that, for instance, although programmes of perceptual motor training are mentioned in Chapter 1, there are no details given. This is because programmes designed by Kephart, Cratty and others are well presented elsewhere; details are given in the list of suggested reading. Some other areas which are included may appear to physical educationalists as fringe activities not central to the core of their subject. The physical educationalists who have contributed to the book feel that their prime concern is to help children to develop to their full potential. If a child's body isn't quite 'standard' in some way we must search diligently to find activities which will help a child feel 'at home' in his body and help him to enjoy bodily experiences. Most activities suggested in these pages can be enjoyed by children with varying needs and abilities, though some are designed to fulfil particular needs. For example, children with communication difficulties are helped particularly by participation in relationship-play, but not all such children are found in schools for the severely educationally subnormal. Similarly, though a creative dance programme is described particularly in relation to mildly educationally subnormal children, much of the material may be used with children who are hard-of-hearing or who have a physical handicap.

The integration of handicapped children into the wider community is a lively educational issue; throughout this book and particularly in the last chapter the reader's attention is drawn to ways of enabling groups or individuals to join others in physical activity. Increasingly, teachers in comprehensive and primary schools find themselves with one or more handicapped children in their class. At present such children tend to be offered a much less satisfying physical education programme than their peers in special schools. They must somehow be given the chance to enjoy movement. We hope this book can help spur our colleagues on to provide this opportunity.

1 Physical education as part of the total education of handicapped children

LILIAN GROVES

Sound education is the art of helping human beings of all ages to grow and develop to a fuller stature of mind, body and spirit, and to live well in their world.

L. Arnaud Reid

Physical education has an important part to play in helping children develop in stature of mind and spirit as well as body; children with 'special needs' may be helped to 'live well in their world' even if that world is more limited than that of their more fortunate peers.

It is of course true to say that every child has the same basic needs – food and shelter, affection, security, self-respect and acceptance. Every child 'needs' to be recognised as a person in his own right. Yet some children come into the school system with considerable deprivations, and in this sense they have very special needs which must be satisfied if they are to develop their full potential as adults. Some children are deprived by the very love their parents have for them, for many physically handicapped children are overprotected, and their development thus is limited because they are denied opportunities to explore their environment. Most children find joy in movement; parents and child together delight in the child's first steps; older children enjoy rolling, climbing and sliding. Unfortunately many children do not experience the thrill of physical challenge because their locomotive powers are severely limited, because they have impaired sensory perception or because their home circumstances restrict physical play. Some, who are free to play with other children, suffer the frustration of exclusion from childhood games.

Whatever the educational situation, we should seek to give children the joys and excitement of physical activity and play in some form. We should use this natural childhood activity to give handicapped children as much opportunity as possible for independence and for acceptance by other children.

A teenage girl subject to frequent and unexplained fainting fits, very withdrawn and apparently unable to cope in an educationally subnormal (moderate) school, was gradually drawn into a twice-weekly dance lesson. After ten weeks she wrote in her diary, 'I feel bootiful when I dans.' Her class teacher at about the same time recorded, 'No fainting fits for four weeks now. She has become more part of the class. She seems less frightened to approach the others and talks more. Attention span improving.' Then she added, 'She actually smiled at me today.'

A group of teachers watched a videotape of older boys working with little ones in a movement session held in a hospital school for the severely retarded. Only as the film drew to a close did the audience realise that the 'older boys' were young men who had been institutionalised for most of their lives. They had previously enjoyed a movement programme of the type described by Veronica Sherborne in another chapter of this book. At that time they had worked with local sixth formers. When the videotape was made they drew upon their experience in movement classes to work with young children. Those who watched the tape were impressed by the outstanding sense of dignity demonstrated by these young men and by their sensitive handling of the young ones.

A visitor was challenged by a group of lively teenagers to an obstacle race. The boys fell about laughing as their visitor, a physical education specialist, attempted without conspicuous success to manoeuvre a wheelchair between posts. Then the 'physically handicapped' youngsters demonstrated their skill in balancing their chairs on two wheels, delicately moving in and out of the obstacles.

In each of these cases an aspect of physical education played an important part in helping young people with different problems reach 'a fuller stature of mind, body and spirit'.

What is meant by physical education?

In recent years there has been much discussion on the meaning and purpose of 'physical education', especially amongst those who teach the new academic courses in colleges and universities. Those who wish to become familiar with the academics' debate on the concept of physical education should read articles such as those by Carlisle and Adams (1969), or the work of Arnold (1968).

For the purpose of this discussion it is perhaps sufficient to say that the term 'physical education' may be taken to mean that aspect of education which makes use of organised physical activities to help achieve the aims of education. These activities take place not only in the gymnasium or hall but on the playing field, in the swimming pool and the sports hall. They include adventure activities taught in the wider environment – on fells, rivers, lakes and even the sea. Most activities, but by no means all, have a competitive element; most, but by no means all, are concerned with big muscle activity. Physical education has rightly been described as not only education *of* the physical but also education *through* the physical.

Almost since the beginning of compulsory education there has been provision for some kind of physical activity. In the early days in elementary schools this was known as 'drill' and later as 'physical training'. Both 'training' and 'drill' imply the disciplining of the body through activities and routines imposed from outside. Physical education – if the term 'education' is to mean anything – cannot imply the type of training given to circus animals or the moulding of an individual into a narrowly preconceived form. Rather, physical education implies the full involvement of the learner in the process; a process which is individualised and is seen as the foundation of a full and satisfying life.

Some physical educationalists think that the highly structured, teacher-directed types of programme advocated by Kephart and his followers cannot be considered part of physical education since they are concerned with training rather than with educating. Yet this type of work has greatly enriched the lives of many handicapped children. If a child's difficulties in co-ordination are so pronounced that he cannot benefit from the more usual forms of physical education or if a child's learning difficulties are very severe then a teacher-directed programme of perceptual motor training may be essential. Most children requiring special education, except the most severely mentally handicapped, want to take part in physical activities recognisably similar to those enjoyed by society at large – swimming, football, athletics, dancing, canoeing and so on. Consequently the emphasis in this book is on activity rather than on handicap. However, physical educationalists should not hold too narrow a view of their subject; nor should teachers with limited training in the subject fall into the trap of embracing a particular 'system' either because it is so highly structured or because it appears delightfully open-ended. No system holds all the answers. The wise teacher will attempt over a period of time to give his pupils a balanced programme involving traditional activities (or at least a selection of the most appropriate), movement exploration, creative and aesthetic experiences and individually planned programmes of sensory motor training. Each approach has something special to offer and a teacher can weight his programme to satisfy the needs of the moment.

Attitudes to physical education

In spite of its long tradition and in spite of what appears so obvious to physical educationalists and interested teachers, the value of physical education, no matter what 'system' it embraces, is not yet universally acknowledged. Just as in the education of highly intelligent children physical education is frequently pushed out of the curriculum in favour of extra examination subjects, it is sometimes displaced in the programme for slow learners in favour of extra remedial reading. For physically handicapped children physiotherapy is sometimes thought to be sufficient.

A survey was carried out in 1973 to examine provisions for physical education in schools for the educationally subnormal (moderate) [ESN(M)] in seven local authorities (Groves, 1975). Most schools offered some physical education though there was a desperate shortage of teachers with more than very minimal experience in PE especially amongst women teachers. Heads wanted more specialist or semi-specialists particularly to work with girls of secondary school age. Only two from a sample of twenty-four head teachers were antagonistic towards the subject. One wrote that he doubted the value of compulsory physical education and that 'Certainly in ESN schools it would never be missed.' The other wrote, 'During twenty years with ESN children I have found that indoor PE is not well done, is not popular and because of the vast range of physical abilities (and disabilities) a sufficiently homogeneous group is difficult to achieve.' I hope that this chapter will show other heads and teachers why it is important to include physical education in the school programme and that the rest of the book will show how it may be 'well done' and 'liked'. Yet another head teacher of an ESN school, while not opposed to PE on principle, wrote that in his school it was a 'cinderella' subject 'pushed out by academic pressures'. But as we shall see there is substantial evidence that reading problems and problems of motor co-ordination are linked – for this reason alone this head should have welcomed physical education. (In fact an interesting programme was later established in this school.)

Most head teachers in the survey spoke of the importance to their children of a well-run physical education programme. One wrote: 'Physical activity, especially where there is non-competitive group participation, provides an opportunity for whole-child development and can add to the colour and quality of life.'

Body–mind relationship

The idea that physical well-being and motor skill has impact upon other aspects of life and adds to the quality of life is not new. The Latin tag 'mens sana in corpore sano' has been the watchword of others besides professional physical educationalists. The Greeks emphasised the importance of balance and harmony of mind and body. Socrates stated 'It is a matter of common knowledge that grave mistakes can often be traced to bad health.' But from time to time since the fifth century BC there has been the notion that one can educate the mind of man and ignore his body. This idea persists today in the teaching of educational philosophers such as R.S. Peters and his followers, who appear to think of man as an intellectual being without a body and perhaps without a soul. None the less twentieth-century doctors are very aware of the psychosomatic unity of man and acknowledge not only that the body may influence the mind but that the mind can have tremendous impact upon the body.

Interestingly, the work of Goldman, an innovator in the field of religious education, also recognises the influence of the body upon man's total development. He believes that a child's physical development and skill and the fearlessness of his approach to life are important in the development of faith.

The Department of Education and Science's pamphlet *The Education of Maladjusted Children* (1975) illustrates the influence of a disturbed mind upon bodily posture and physical well being:

Many maladjusted children show most obviously the influence of an unhappy mind upon the body. When they are admitted too many of them are weedy with hang-dog appearance, slouching and tense as if they expected to be attacked.

And the Department's pamphlet *Physical Education for the Physically Handicapped* (1971) illustrates the reverse:

The need for bodily activity is equally vital for the child with a physical handicap . . . He is, moreover, deprived by the very fact of his disability of the sensory and exploratory activities on which depend his later development, his liveliness, his curiosity and his interests.

Before going on to look further at the inter-relationship of different aspects of 'self' we should consider the more obvious aspect of physical activity – that of its importance for health and physical fitness. There is well-documented research of the direct correlation between a sedentary life and premature degenerative heart disease. Almost inevitably handicapped people lead an even more sedentary life than the general public and thus for them it is even more important to 'educate for fitness' from early childhood. Unfortunately physical fitness while at school is not 'money in the bank' for adult life, and children should learn the need for life-long exercise habits. Even amongst intelligent physically handicapped children there is a tendency to give up medically prescribed exercise once they have left school and the care of the school physiotherapist. But to learn this need is not enough. Each child must be helped to achieve his own potential in movement. A child should be helped to 'feel at home' in his own body, no matter how imperfect that body may be.

However, concern for physical fitness should not blind us to other aspects of the subject. Not all the activities advocated in this book involve the vigorous type of activity essential for real fitness, but physical activity, even of a less vigorous nature, is important for all-round development.

Evidence of the relationship between physical and social development

The relationship between physical ineptness and emotional disturbance was shown in a study carried out in Glasgow and reported by Stott (1966). Delinquent youths were shown to have significantly poorer motor co-ordination than comparable non-delinquents. This could be another illustration of the impact of a disturbed mind upon the body. Equally it could be an illustration of the effect of clumsiness upon mental health.

There is growing concern in the medical profession, as well as amongst educationalists, at the plight of children who are physically clumsy whether or not they are also educationally retarded. Indeed it has been shown that intelligent children who have co-ordination problems are often wrongly classified as of below average intelligence. A consultant neurologist confessed that when a fat, clumsy, obviously depressed boy of about eleven was referred to his clinic he thought he must have a significant mental handicap. His IQ turned out to be 144 though his manner and behaviour suggested that he was very much below average intelligence. The consultant spoke of many children referred to his clinic because of behaviour problems who suffered from very poor co-ordination. The problem of clumsiness is distressing to children of average or above-average intelligence; it can be devastating for those of less intelligence.

In early childhood acceptance by the peer group depends almost entirely on a child's ability to join the group at play. A child unable to run and jump has obvious problems, but so too do children who have difficulty in catching a ball. Such children are often rejected and even mocked by their peers. Well-meaning attempts by teachers or parents to make more skilful children include them in their play can be disastrous. Because some children thus miss out on early group play they incidentally lose the opportunity to become more skilful and so are unlikely at a later stage to be acceptable in team play even at the level of street games. It is, of course, in play that many early and valuable social experiences take place. Awareness of self and feelings of self-esteem are closely linked with bodily experiences. Much will be said later of the value of successful physical experiences in total development. Few physical education books stress the effect of failure in physical activities, yet this can have very long-term results.

Even in a school where academic distinction was deemed more important than athletic prowess Symes (1972) found that clumsy boys were rejected not only in games but in other situations also. He suggested that even a slight motor impairment could interfere with both learning and personality development. Obviously the more serious the impairment the more difficult acceptance by one's peers.

Children who are mentally retarded have even more difficulties in play. Not only, as we shall see, are they likely to have problems of co-ordination, but they may not understand the rules of play.

Oliver and Keog (1967) showed that even amongst educationally subnormal children there is a significant relationship between physical abilities, social acceptance and behaviour patterns. Many physically awkward children are withdrawn and have difficulty in relating to others; some rejected at play become defensive or aggressive.

The answer to this problem is not, of course, to withdraw children from play and so protect them from possible failure and rejection. Teachers, parents and others must do their best to improve children's skills so that they are able to join in group play. There is evidence, as we shall see later, that the physical fitness and motor skills of both mentally handicapped and physically handicapped children can be improved. Evidence will also be presented that those whose skills are so improved can improve in social relationships and in behaviour.

Physical ability and academic progress

Thinking of the psychosomatic unity of man inevitably leads us to question evidence of the relationship between physical and intellectual performance. It has already been said that intelligent children can suffer from difficulties of co-ordination. It is also true that some children with severe physical handicaps have achieved university degrees. These, however, are exceptions. While most studies dealing with the 'normal' population show only a very tenuous relationship between intelligence and physical skill they do indicate a strong link between certain aspects of motor development and school achievement.

For example, Ismail and Gruber (1967) carried out an intensive study of fifth- and sixth-graders in the USA. They used forty-two different items to measure motor and intellectual abilities. Their findings showed that while physical growth was not significantly related to intelligence, co-ordination and rhythm were significantly and positively related to academic achievement. They also found that strength, speed and accuracy of aim, though virtually unrelated to intelligence, did show some relation to academic progress.

A number of studies in this country and the USA have shown that those of low academic standing are seldom involved in school sport. One London study indicated a close connection between academic success (as shown by streaming) and physical performance (as shown by membership of school or house teams). Children in higher streams had a disproportionate number of places in school teams. The study by the National Foundation for Educational Research not only supported these findings but showed that even where comprehensive schools were dedicated to mixed-ability teaching, school teams were made up in much the same way.

These studies simply confirm what most teachers know. Most also appreciate that membership of school teams is not based entirely on physical skill. Competitive play demands the ability to 'read' fast-changing situations, to anticipate the opponent's next move, to adapt one's desires to those of one's team-mates and to keep one's head in face of challenge. A further complication is that where children continuously fail in academic situations they are more likely to reject the whole culture of the school than to seek membership of school teams.

Nevertheless, other studies show a very clear relationship between academic progress and physical ability. The Cheshire Education Committee's report on retarded children (1973) stated that:

> By the time they reach the secondary school, children of low intelligence are generally of poorer physical development and are less physically able than the more intelligent.

The report continues:

Some dull children have excellent co-ordination but the majority suffer from lack of contrast in range and quality of movement and a proneness to accidents because of this clumsiness.

W. Allen, working with a small group of junior-aged boys referred to a remedial centre for protracted failure in reading and writing, found some evidence of a correlation between motor impairment and the ability to read and write commensurate with a child's age and recorded IQ. He found that over 50% suffered from general motor impairment (as defined by Stott, 1966). Half of the boys also suffered from directional confusion and mixed lateral dominance.

Those whose research has been with children in special schools have found similar relationships. Gulliford (1966) found a connection between difficulties over body and space awareness and reversal problems in language. The investigations of Lunt (1973) and others indicated a clear relationship between poor progress in reading and difficulties in rhythm as well as in space awareness.

Other studies show that children who are academically retarded are also retarded in a wide range of physical skills. Rarick and Dobbins (1973) and others have all indicated that amongst retarded children the greater the mental retardation the poorer the level of physical skill.

The work of Rarick and Dobbins showed that educationally mentally retarded children were *as a group* very much poorer than intellectually able children of the same age and sex in motor tasks requiring elements of muscular strength and power, gross and fine motor control, flexibility and balance. However, they also found that in all tests some of the retarded children scored well above the mean for normal children. Teachers working with remedial children in mainstream education will know from observation that this is true. One physical educationalist working in a large streamed comprehensive school has said: 'The lowest streams show a much wider spread of ability than the A streams. These girls range from the highly gifted to the painfully slow.'

The importance of developing to the full the physical potential of those gifted in this field, though they may be educationally retarded, is self-evident. But what of those who are far below the norm? It is hoped to show here that even these children can be helped, and that such help is of far-reaching importance to their future lives. Even more valuable perhaps is attention to the physical needs of handicapped children at a very young age. The importance of motor experiences in early childhood for later intellectual development is well established in the work of Piaget, Kephart and others. Kephart (1960) has said: 'Motor patterns are the foundation for more complex learning, because motor patterns provide the basis for meaningful orientation.'

It is clearly important that long before handicapped children enter the formal educational system their parents and nurses give them as many opportunities as possible to develop basic motor skills. Equally obviously, when children with physical handicaps enter the system, time spent improving motor skills and increasing opportunities for locomotion is time well spent. Less obvious perhaps is that one may actually be wasting time trying to teach retarded children academic skills such as reading if they have problems of co-ordination.

> Instead of noting that some children have difficulty in catching a ball or in jumping or skipping, but not doing anything about it because of the pressure to provide adequate reading and spelling attainment, we may do well to develop the basic neuro-muscular skills first (Forbes, 1972).

There exists amongst physical educationalists, as amongst other teachers, some scepticism on the transfer of effect from one situation to another and about the possibility of social or academic outcomes of programmes designed primarily to improve physical skills. The nineteenth-century public school belief that participation in team games brought about desirable character traits is disparaged. The claims of the Outward Bound Movement that participation in outdoor pursuits can improve character are questioned. Much that goes on in the name of 'sport', both professional and amateur, causes many to query the ethics of competitive physical activities. In spite of these queries there are very adequate reasons for supporting physical activity even at a highly competitive level. Here we are concerned with those whose skill is very much below this level; and if one accepts the findings of the studies already mentioned on the relationship amongst handicapped children of physical ability and other aspects of development, then it is not unreasonable to suppose that *if* physical skills can be improved this will have impact upon academic progress and social behaviour. There is evidence that physical skills can be improved and that this improvement will indeed have far-reaching effects.

The effect of additional physical education programmes in the education of handicapped children

The majority of the studies described in this section relate to children with learning difficulties; most concern moderately subnormal children. However, many believe that these findings are applicable to severely retarded children also. Francis and Rarick's study (1960) seems to indicate that the motor abilities of both mildly and severely retarded children are organised similarly to those of normal children and that attainment of these abilities follows the same curve. They therefore conclude that both groups of retarded children may profit from the same kind of motor experiences as normal children, provided the stage of learning is appropriate to their stage of mental development. The same is true of physically handicapped children, though here it may well be necessary to adapt the skill patterns.

In order to test the all-round physical fitness of slow learners before and after an extended period of daily physical education lessons, both Stein (1965) and

Solomon and Prangle (1967) employed the AAHPER (American Association of Health, Physical Education and Recreation) youth fitness test. Both studies showed that with 'blocked' periods of teaching, educationally mentally retarded (i.e. ESN (M)) boys can attain the same fitness levels as their normal peers. Solomon and Prangle re-tested their group after a six-week interval and found that the gains in physical fitness had been retained even though the intensive programme had been discontinued. Of course if the boys had not later continued to exercise, in a relatively short period of time their fitness levels would have dropped.

There is plenty of evidence that motor skills can be improved. Bundschuh *et al.* (1972) showed that much the same technique could be used with both moderately and severely handicapped pupils. He took fourteen severely retarded and twenty-six moderately retarded young people aged 5 to 19 years. After twenty daily swimming lessons involving carefully selected drills taught on a one-to-one basis together with some free play, 90% of the class could swim at least six feet, compared with only three who could swim this far before the programme began. Not only did all the moderately retarded learn to swim: over 10% went from being non-swimmers to being able to swim over seventy-five feet!

The studies which follow show that not only can skills be taught and fitness improved but also that when this happens it has an effect upon other aspects of the personality.

One of the earliest British studies and one which set the pattern for many which followed was that carried out by Oliver in 1958. In the so-called Packwood experiment he took a group of ESN (M) boys from a residential school and gave them a very substantial programme of physical activity every day for ten weeks. Scores in tests of physical achievement, intellectual and emotional development were compared with those of a control group. In all three areas the experimental group made significant gains. Oliver's findings have been criticised on the grounds that he made no provision for the 'Hawthorne Effect'. ('Hawthorne Effect' is the term commonly used to describe the phenomenon of improved test scores brought about by the subjects' realisation that they are involved in an experimental situation.) Oliver acknowledged the probable influence of a feeling of importance amongst the experimental group but also attributed the gains to a combination of the effect of achievement and success, improved adjustment and improved physical condition. In the nineteen sixties a number of studies attempted to reproduce the Packwood experiment while making allowances for the Hawthorne Effect. With very few exceptions the findings agreed with those of Oliver.

One of the more extensive studies was that carried out by Rarick and Broadhead (1968). This American study examined the role of physical education in the modification of the motor, intellectual, social and emotional behaviour of 275 educationally retarded and 206 brain-damaged children of primary-school age. One control group followed a special art programme; two groups followed special physical activity programmes and one group, also acting as a control, followed its normal programme. The children were all taken for their special activity by their own class teacher for one period every school day for twenty weeks. Rarick and Broadhead reported that children participating in both the specially prepared experimental programmes showed statistically significant improvement in scores of motor, intellectual and emotional development compared with the control group. In other words, the special art programme produced the same sort of all-round improvement as did the physical education programme. The important aspect was, as Oliver pointed out in his Packwood experiment, the promotion of feelings of achievement and success.

Many experiences may be used to promote these feelings, but it is probably easier to make children aware of success (and, of course, failure) in physical activity than in any other. Physical experiences are immediate; feedback is almost instantaneous. Anyone who has watched a child – or an adult – become 'waterborne' for the first time does not need telling how immediate and overwhelming is the moment of triumph.

The children taking part in Rarick and Broadhead's physical education programmes showed, as one would expect, greater improvement in motor performance than did the children in the other groups. A particularly interesting finding was that the girls did not show improvement in behaviour to anything like the same extent as the boys.

One does not expect to find in adolescent or immediately pre-adolescent girls, regardless of intellectual ability, the same interest in physical activities as in generally shown by boys. The Schools' Council Working Paper 11: 'Society and the Young School-Leaver' (1967) and other studies produced evidence of the importance to adolescent boys of physical activity but indicated that it is of much less interest to girls. However there is evidence that when an activity is chosen which is of particular interest to girls then the success experienced can have the same impact upon other aspects of life as described for boys by Oliver and others.

Dance in particular has considerable appeal for girls. The work of Bruce with handicapped children using dance programmes is well known. She visited many schools in this country and America and found that where dance flourished so too did lively written work and expressive paintings. In a lecture at the 1973 PEA conference she said that in her experience

> dance has been the opening pathway to so many activities – to music, to painting, to the awareness of shape, to relationships and to words.

Others have reported similar improvement, particularly in attitudes, as a result of dance programmes. Neal (1964) reported on a research project in Australia in which children aged eight to nine years and with IQ's ranging from 36 to 62 had regular dance lessons for five months. A control group had normal physical activity in unstructured 'play' periods. Neal reported that the experimental group

> developed a cohesion and camaraderie which one usually considers indicative of higher levels of intellectual functioning.

In an Israeli study dance was used with children whose ability was limited by a difficult environment. The research, reported by Friedman-Witthower (1971), involved two groups of nine- and ten-year-olds from 'culturally deprived' homes. The groups were carefully matched to produce an experimental group which had four lessons of 'movement' and dance a week for two years and a control group which had no special dance programme. The members of the experimental group were reported as showing a marked rise in IQ, in body and space awareness and in their relationship with others. Friedman-Witthower declared:

> Well-guided movement education helps to overcome developmental blocks, influences positively certain character-qualities, leads, apart from better motor performance, to better scholastic achievement and is fundamentally important in the rehabilitation of culturally deprived children.

Unfortunately, as in many of the other studies described, details of actual teaching programme were not included in reports on the project. Again, however, there was great emphasis on the effect of physical 'success' upon the self-esteem of the children and upon increased readiness to tackle both physical and mental tasks.

Many children in ESN (M) schools and in remedial streams of comprehensive schools are there largely as a result of difficult home backgrounds. (See for example Wiseman (1964) and Williams and Gruber (1967).) These children have rejected the 'culture of the book' and must find success elsewhere.

One experimental programme of dance was taken with adolescent girls from three different special schools, at least one of which had a high proportion of girls who fell into this category (Groves, 1975). The programme was based on the belief that lessons in dance would be attractive to adolescent girls, that it was possible to structure dance so that there would be little opportunity for failure, and that if particular attention was given to partner and group work this would lead to improved relations within the group. The schools used in this study varied greatly: one had many children with physical handicaps; one had a high proportion of children from broken homes; one had a very high proportion of children who were borderline severely retarded. The programme followed with each group was similar and is discussed in Chapter 3. Here it is the statistical findings in the tests which are of interest.

Behaviour was evaluated by an adaptation of the Bristol Social Adjustment Guides. Questions in the test related to:

1. *Unforthcomingness* (defined by Stott (1966) as 'inhibited behaviour, defensiveness against anybody or anything strange, not against affection in general')
2. *Restlessness* or distractability
3. *Aggression*
4. *Social isolation*

Stott reports that 'unforthcomingness' is the predominant form of behaviour disturbance found amongst backward children. Several of the children in this experiment were regarded by their teachers as very aggressive and a number had been transferred from comprehensive and secondary modern schools largely because of their violent anti-social behaviour.

Following the dance programmes the girls, as a group, were judged by their class teachers as greatly improved in behaviour, particularly in the areas of 'restlessness' and 'unforthcomingness'. Children who show restlessness are described by Stott as attending to nothing for more than a few minutes and as failing to conceptualise. Following the experimental programmes two of the class teachers expressed their astonishment at the increase in the length of time the girls were able and willing to concentrate in a variety of situations. The amount of aggression shown by the girls was much less following successful participation in dance. The control group on the other hand had significantly worse scores in the behaviour tests than they had at the beginning of the experimental period. This was expected since the scores were based on the class teachers' assessment of pupils and were taken at the beginning and end of term. One would expect teachers to judge behaviour more harshly when tired at the end of term than they would at the start of term. This made the improvement found in the experimental groups of even more interest.

Still more interesting, perhaps, was the clear change of attitude from 'I can't' to 'I can'. Many girls in one group refused to put pen or paint to paper without 'guide lines'. By the end of the programme of dance they were almost all painting very freely, though no formal instruction had been given. Not only did lively paintings arise from the dance lessons, but dances were sometimes inspired by the girls' paintings.

After two terms of successful participation in dance one fourteen-year-old went to her class teacher and said, 'Well, now you'd better teach me to read.' She made rapid progress. There is of course no evidence to prove that this was a direct result of the dance programme but certainly this girl, who had previously shown little interest in any aspect of school and was indeed a frequent truant, became much more highly motivated following successful participation in creative dance. After the experiment was concluded one school held an open day. Dancers, including several girls who previously had been very withdrawn, took part in a performance. One parent with tears in her eyes expressed her delight over the change in her daughter's manner.

The study made use of sociometric techniques in an attempt to find statistical evidence of the cohesion of the group and an individual's acceptability to her peers. In the groups which had followed a dance programme fewer girls were rejected than at first and none was unchosen in the second test. In the control group the same number were unchosen in both tests but there was a considerable increase in the number actively rejected in the second test.

These findings point towards agreement with Frostig's statement on the value of 'creative movement'. She said:

> Educators have at their disposal one of the most powerful means of enhancing their pupils' awareness of themselves and of the world and of simultaneously enhancing their emotional and social development. The experiences gained through the creative activity heighten the individual's awareness of his own feelings, provide inner satisfaction and a sense of accomplishment and give new meaning to life (Frostig, 1970).

Certainly for girls dance seems to have a great deal to offer to all-round development. The two foreign studies previously described included some junior-age boys. Some British research is at present looking at the part which dance has to play in the education of secondary-age boys in special schools.

Other aspects of the physical education curriculum have been shown to bring about similar changes in social adjustment. In one programme Goodwin (1970) compared the effects of two different approaches. One group of educationally retarded children was taken for group-oriented activities of a traditional nature while a matched group had an individualised programme of movement exploration. Each group had 30 minutes a day five days a week for ten weeks. Goodwin found that both groups had improved scores in tests of physical fitness, intelligence and social maturity. He found however that the group following a traditional programme made greater gains in physical fitness tests while those following the movement exploration programme had higher gains in the IQ test. This is as one might expect since the pupil was asked to make his own decisions and to work out problems in the movement exploration programme, but could not spend as much time in active performance as was allowed in the more directed programme.

A group of educationally retarded boys was taken for twelve weeks of judo instruction. Davis and Byrd (1975) tested the boys by means of the California Test of Personality, the Wide-Range Achievement Test and the AAHPER Special Fitness Test (i.e. a test specifically intended for use with handicapped children). Subjecting the results to statistical analysis they found that there were significant changes in total adjustment and in some measures of fitness. One particular case was of special interest. He was completely withdrawn, spoke to no one, showed no emotion and was completely uninterested in life. Before the end of the twelve-week programme this boy was assisting the slower learners at judo and was at the end of the experimental period elected captain of the judo team.

Davis suggests that 'these gains were attributed in part to breaking the well-established repeated failure pattern'.

Emphasis in all these programmes has been on 'success'. It is perhaps important to say at this stage that, just as it is important to give all children successful experiences, it is equally important to help them to accept failure: one cannot go through life protected from this. Some teachers are strongly opposed to competition. One special school head in the survey mentioned earlier said: 'Inter-school games bring out the worst in children at all levels and should be abolished.' Others believed equally strongly that it was good for youngsters to face up to being beaten. One head of a residential school for physically handicapped children encourages his pupils not only to take part in the disabled programme at Stoke Mandeville and to compete in special school sports, but also to play in the local junior football league, even though they play in wheelchairs and adapt the rules. Children in this school are amongst those referred to in Chapter 5, on adventure activities. They show great physical courage and determination; they encourage one another to improve their physical skills; the more able help the less able to have successful experiences; and by the time these young people reach the senior part of the school most of them are well able to cope with competition. First, however, must come confidence in their own skill.

A consideration of the research relevant to the contribution of PE to the development of handicapped children cannot conclude without reference to the work of Kephart, Doman and their followers. The programmes of perceptual motor training devised by Kephart and others are widely used with children who have severe learning difficulties. This work is clearly related to Piaget's theories of concept foundation in the young child. Spectacular results have been claimed. One head teacher wrote:

> I have sixty of the most severely handicapped children in the county and this aspect of our work (i.e. Kephart's programme) is proving unbelievably valuable in helping severely handicapped children to perceive shapes, with hand–eye co-ordination etc.

There is empirical evidence that individually designed perceptual motor programmes of this nature can indeed bring about the improvements this headmaster described, and in doing so significantly improve the self-concept of adolescents. There is also evidence that such programmes may significantly improve the social development of mentally retarded children. (See for example Loewendahl and Richard (1966) and Cortazzo (1964).)

So we are on firm ground in claiming that many aspects of physical education have very substantial impact on the all-round development of handicapped children. The type of programme which is most successful will depend on the interest and skill of the teacher as well as on the particular abilities of the children. The danger of embracing one particular system has already been touched on, and the desirability of a mixed programme mentioned. On the whole it would appear that there is likely to be more impact upon intellectual functioning where children are actively engaged in decision-making in the physical education lesson; children are more likely to develop social skills where there is opportunity to work together with others – even initially on a one-to-one basis; they are likely to be less restless in the classroom if there has been opportunity to become completely absorbed in a physical activity; and they are more likely to develop sensitivity to the needs of others and become less aggressive when others have been in some way dependent on them. Fitness is likely to improve and with it the opportunity to enjoy life more fully where activities are physically demanding; motivation is likely to be heightened where feedback is immediate and success obvious to both performer and those who watch; and a more active leisure life, more chance to enjoy life is likely where activities can be linked to those of the wider community.

This chapter gives but a sample of the growing body of research which shows that handicapped children do indeed have very special needs which can be at least partially satisfied by some or all of the wealth of activities which are included under the umbrella of physical education. Those responsible for educating handicapped children who ignore this aspect of education will be depriving many of their pupils of the opportunity 'to grow and develop to a fuller stature . . . and to live well in their world'.

Selected bibliography related to research

Arnold, P. *Education, Physical Education and Personality Development.* Heinemann, 1968

Bruce, V. *Awakening the Slower Mind.* Pergamon, 1969

Bundschuh, E.L. *et al.* 'Teaching the retarded to swim', *Mental Retardation*, 10 Mar. 1972

Carlisle, R. and Adams, M. 'The concept of PE', and 'A reply', *Proceedings of Conference of Philosophy of Education Society*, 1969

Cortazzo, A.D. 'Increasing sociability for the retarded through activity programmes', *Journal of Rehabilitation*, 30 Feb. 1964

Davis, B. and Byrd, R.J. 'The effects of judo on EMR boys', *Journal of Sports Medicine and Physical Fitness*, XV, **4**, Dec. 1975

DES. *Report 47: The Education of Maladjusted Children.* 1975

Forbes, G.K. 'Learning and the importance of neuro-muscular development', *Discover*, Dec. 1972

Francis, R.J. and Rarick, G. 'Motor characteristics of the mentally retarded', Research Monograph No. 1, US Dept of Health, Education and Welfare, 1960

Friedman-Witthower, E.D. 'The influence of movement upon culturally deprived children', *Gymnasion*, VIII, **1**, Spring 1971

Frostig, M. and Maslow, P. *Movement Education: Theory and Practice*, Follet, Chicago, 1970

Goodwin, L.A. 'The effects of two selected PE programmes on trainable men-

tally retarded children', PhD Thesis, University of Utah, 1970; summary in *Challenge*, VII, **1**, Sept.–Oct. 1971
Groves, L. 'Physical education for slow-learning girls in north-east schools with special reference to the effect of creative dance on behaviour and friendship patterns amongst adolescent ESN (M) girls', M.Ed. Thesis, Durham University, 1975
Gulliford, R. *Backwardness and Educational Failure*. National Foundation for Educational Research, London, 1966
Ismail, A.H. and Gruber, J.J. *Motor Aptitudes and Intellectual Performance*. Merrill Books, Ohio, 1967
Kephart, N.C. *The Slow Learner in the Classroom*. Merrill Books, Ohio, 1960
Loewendahl, E. and Richard, T.W. 'A therapeutic approach to adolescence', *Journal of the Association for Physical and Mental Rehabilitation*, 20 Feb. 1966
Lunt, I. 'Rhythm and the slow learner', *Special Education*, LXIV, **4**, 1973
Neal, A.D. 'The effect of a broad art and movement programme', International Congress of the Scientific Study of Mental Deficiency, Copenhagen, 1964
Oliver, J.N. 'The effect of physical condition in exercises and activities on mental characteristics of ESN boys', *British Journal of Educational Psychology*, **28**, 1958
Oliver, N. and Keog, J.F. 'Helping the physically awkward', *Special Education*, LVI, **1**, 1967
Rarick, G. and Broadhead, G.D. 'The effect of individualized versus group-oriented PE programs on selected parameters of the development of EMR and MBD children', Report of the Dept of PE, University of Wisconsin, Madison, 1968
Rarick, G. and Dobbins, D.A. 'Basic components in the motor performance of EMR children: implications for curriculum development', Research Report, University of California, Berkeley, 1973
Solomon, A. and Prangle, R. 'Demonstrating physical fitness improvement in EMR children', *Exceptional Children*, Nov. 1967
Stein, J. 'Physical fitness of mentally retarded boys relative to national age norms', *Rehabilitation Literature*, 26 July 1965
Stott, D.H. *Studies of Troublesome Children*. Tavistock, 1966
Symes, K. 'Clumsiness and sociometric status of intellectually gifted boys', *Bulletin of Physical Education*, BAOLPE, XI, Apr. 1972
Williams, P. and Gruber, E. *Response to Special Schooling*. Longmans, 1967
Wiseman, S. *Education and Environment*. Manchester University Press, 1964

2 Movement for developmentally retarded children

VERONICA SHERBORNE

Mentally handicapped children are very different from children who are physically handicapped and from those children described as educationally subnormal (moderate) who have failed the normal educational system. Mentally handicapped or educationally subnormal (severe) children are born with some dysfunction of the nervous system or may suffer from chromosome irregularity (Down's Syndrome). Some children may appear normal until perhaps the age of two, when it is realised the child is showing autistic tendencies, the cause of which is still unknown. Others may become mentally handicapped as a result of a road accident or a severe illness which has damaged the brain. All mentally handicapped children are retarded and function at the level of a much younger child; those in 'special care' classes for multiply handicapped children may function in a way that is appropriate for an infant. A more able mentally handicapped child may function physically and socially close to the level of a normal child of his age but may behave emotionally in a younger manner, and may be intellectually at a still younger level. This is disconcerting for the teacher who is used to normal children, but presents an interesting challenge to the teacher who is experienced in assessing the abilities and needs of individual mentally handicapped children and in planning and carrying out a programme of learning experiences designed for each child.

Although usually there are not more than ten children to a class in a school for ESN (S) children it may contain children with an extremely wide range of abilities. Some children may suffer from varying degrees of spasticity, others may have impaired sight or partial hearing and some may be extremely disturbed. On the whole mentally handicapped children are affectionate and responsive and their teacher is rewarded for his efforts by their progress.

Until 1971 mentally handicapped children were described as 'ineducable' and were in the care of the Ministry of Health in training centres; since that date they have become the responsibility of the Department of Education and Science and are taught in special schools designated as Educationally Subnormal (Severe). Increasingly such schools have pupils with emotional problems including hyperactive children, children with autistic tendencies and severely socially deprived children, some of whom may have been referred from schools for mildly educationally subnormal children.

A great deal of research is being carried out in many countries in the field of developmental psychology with particular reference to the development of severely retarded children. Teachers working with handicapped children need to have a good understanding of the developmental processes in the normal child, particularly between birth and the age of five.

I have found that the challenges set by mentally handicapped children have helped me to understand better the needs of normal children and even adults.

Although we are learning more and more about the developmental processes and their relation to the education of mentally handicapped children, we still do not succeed in helping each child use all his resources and achieve his potential. Most mentally handicapped children are learning through sensory–motor processes and because of their retardation have not been able to benefit from early sensory and motor experiences. As they grow older they need constant reinforcement of these experiences – otherwise lack of stimulus may lead to secondary retardation.

Any group of mentally handicapped children shows a wide range of physical aptitudes and limitations; some children are almost as skilful as normal children while others have considerable difficulty in performing simple physical tasks. They all benefit from physical activity, which can range from physiotherapy for the profoundly handicapped to the skilled use of conventional gymnastic equipment by the more able children. A physical education programme should include developmental movement, work with both large and small apparatus, swimming, outdoor activities, games, riding, movement to music and social dance. Of these activities swimming is particularly beneficial both for profoundly handicapped children and for those who are physically able. Other chapters deal with many of these activities. (See also Sherborne in *Physical and Creative Activities for the Severely Mentally Handicapped*, G. Upton, ed., Cambridge University Press, 1979.) In this chapter I shall describe the aspect of education which is particularly significant in the development of mentally retarded children: the development of relationship and communication through movement experiences.

The first task of the teacher is to establish her relationship with each child. I suggest to student teachers that they get to know the children in the classroom, particularly winning the confidence of more disruptive pupils before embarking on a movement class. I also recommend that teachers begin by taking short movement sessions in the more enclosed space of the classroom before using the school hall. The teacher lays the foundations of a good relationship through being physically involved with the children.

Many of the children will be functioning in some respects like three-year-olds, so their teacher needs to join in the movement class and play with them. At the same time a teacher must be firm when the need arises. Like all children mentally retarded children respond to the personality of adults and will test a new teacher or student and 'play up' if they think they can get away with it.

Many children will not have experienced play with adults before coming to school. Those who have tend to be much more confident than other children. Children who have opportunities for regular relationship play in school become more physically confident and more sociable. They build up a good relationship with their teacher, and with the teacher's aide, if there is one, and they are likely to function much better in a group.

Some children need play on a one-to-one basis and there are a number of ways of organising this. An increasing number of schools arrange for older mentally handicapped children to work with younger children in school, to the advantage of both groups. The older children need help with developing their own movement vocabulary and resources first so that they bring something special to partner work. In one school I saw bright little children of five and six, mostly Down's Syndrome children, working with adolescent special care children who were multiply handicapped. Three of the younger children working together were able to pull a tall fifteen-year-old along as he lay on the floor and give him a slide.

In some schools which cater for both groups older ESN (M) children may partner younger ESN (S) children. Chapter 9 describes ways in which children from comprehensive schools can help with this work. The experience benefits all those involved.

Types of relationship play

1. Complete support

When an adult takes the weight of a child and supports him the child experiences this both physically and psychologically. Being carried, rocked, hugged are significant sensory–motor experiences for the young baby; if the quality of support the adult gives the child is caring and warm the child feels secure with the adult and develops security within himself. The mentally handicapped child who will not trust his weight to the adult shows not so much lack of confidence in the adult as lack of confidence in himself. When a child allows himself to be supported by an adult he demonstrates that he trusts himself and is prepared to commit himself to a relationship with the adult.

A child's weight may be fully or partially supported. A child sitting beside an adult on the floor and leaning against him is experiencing support. The child who dares not trust his weight to an adult will probably not trust his weight to the floor either; he may refuse to lie down or if he does lie his head will be raised anxiously off the floor.

In the early stages a child will enjoy sitting on or astride an adult who sits or lies on the floor and will feel superior and confident. The adult can respond by giving the child a ride on his back, keeping flat on the ground (if the child is not too heavy) or the adult can lie on his back and bounce the child gently on his stomach. The aim is to give the child an enjoyable experience so that he wants to continue the relationship.

The adult, on all fours, can carry the child on his back in different ways. The child can lie face down on the adult's back, gripping with arms round his neck, and with legs round his body; as the 'horse' sways a little the child holds on. The child can sit as if on a horse, and as confidence grows will lie with his back against the adult's back and relax while he sways gently. A child can also lie face down across the adult's back and be carried off by the adult on all fours. With the adult sitting on the floor, knees bent and feet on the ground, the child can sit on the adult's knees, or lie along them, and confident children enjoy standing on the adult's knees and holding his hands for balance.

Children enjoy slithering over the adult, who may be lying face down or kneeling on all fours. They enjoy somersaulting over and round the adult's back when he is on all fours, and over his shoulder when he is sitting with legs stretched out in front, leaving a space between them in which the child's body unrolls.

In many of these activities the child feels his back and stomach in contact with the adult's body. It is extremely important that the child moves the centre of his body in a flexible lively way and that he becomes aware of the movement of his trunk. So often this central part of the body is stiff and the child is unaware of having a middle which connects his lower limbs to his upper extremities. In the early stages children benefit from movement of the body as a whole.

It is valuable for the child to climb over and under the adult's body. The adult can kneel up on one knee with the foot of the other leg firmly placed on the floor to make a steady base. The child can climb and crawl up and round and down and through spaces made by the adult's body, using the adult's arms as the branches of a tree. This kind of play must be done while the child is small enough for the adult to manage, but heavier older children can be helped by having two people on all fours, side by side, for climbing over and crawling under.

It is interesting to see which children will cling on to the adult, because this is a clear indication of willingness to be involved with the adult.

2. Support with free flow of body weight

The simplest example of this is for the adult to sit on the floor behind the child with the child between his legs. Using his whole body, arms, trunk and thighs, the adult gently rocks the child from side to side. The child must tip off balance if his weight is to be given to the adult to support. Most mentally handicapped children like being contained and rocked; the support and free flow express a caring, feeling relationship which is particularly enjoyed by Down's Syndrome children. Some disturbed children find that a relationship which is gentle and tender is threatening, and other disturbed children, who like free-flow movement, are sometimes afraid to be enclosed by the adult.

Rocking sideways can be changed to more energetic rocking where the adult, with the child on his lap, falls backwards onto the adult's back, then rocks forward to sitting again. The adult can lie on his back with knees bent and held up and hold the child above him across his shins, his hands supporting the child's shoulders; this gives the child the sensation of flying. In this position a child who normally avoids eye contact will often look down at his partner. In all these activities the free-flow movement should be accompanied by appropriate humming, singing or speaking sounds which reinforce the movement experience and make the activities more fun.

Children enjoy being bounced, another weight-flow activity, and the adult can make his body into a variety of mini-trampettes. Most children enjoy all kinds of swinging. Two adults, each holding the wrist and ankle of a child between them, can swing the child in a safe and pleasant way. An adult can pick up a child by holding him under the arms, the child facing away, and swing him round, or can hold him by wrist and ankle and sweep him round over the surface of the floor. Some very disturbed children will allow physical support from an adult only because they enjoy the sensation of being swung so much, and this can be a useful way of breaking through a child's resistance to being physically involved with anyone.

Jumping is another activity which involves the free flow of weight. An adult can help a child to jump by supporting him under the elbows as he stands facing the adult and use his own voice to co-ordinate the child's jump and his lift.

Through the free-flow movements of rocking, swinging, bouncing and jumping we can feed enjoyable, harmonious, whole-body experiences into children who are tense and anxious; their faces relax and express surprise and amusement; they begin to trust adults, and to enjoy playing. On the other hand hyperactive children can become more excited if movement is too abandoned, so the adult has to be skilful in combining free-flow experiences with other more earthing and stabilising experiences.

3. Mutual support: balancing weight

This is a more advanced aspect of supporting in that adult and child are supporting one another and depending on each other. The least demanding form of this sharing relationship is seen when two people make a see-saw together. Both sit on the floor facing each other holding wrists, and take it in turn to lie backwards, head touching the floor, and then help the partner to lie back. Some adolescents can sit back to back and by pushing hard with their feet against the ground they can stand up and sit down together, keeping their backs in contact. An adult can help a child experience this mutual balance and shared support by standing firmly based with knees slightly bent. The adult and child hold each other's wrists, the child stands on the adult's thighs and the two lean back holding a rather spectacular balance. All balancing requires the child to 'listen' to his own body and to his partner's body at the same time. With good teaching some mentally handicapped children can achieve this.

4. Containing

An adult can make his body into a variety of containing 'houses' by sitting on the floor, using his arms to make the walls of the 'house', by kneeling on all fours, or by balancing on his hands and feet, hips up in the air. Most children need and enjoy the security which comes from being contained and rocked at the same time. Some children who are threatened by being contained may accept it if it is done lightly and because the adult is out of sight behind the child. Containing can also be expressed as a strong hug and the 'house' can turn into a 'prison'. Most children enjoy the struggle to get free and benefit from this because they experience their strength against an adult. Some children find being closely held so comforting that they do not want to escape.

The most outspoken expression of containing is experienced when an adult stands with a firm base, knees slightly bent, arms open, and the child runs towards her and leaps up gripping with legs round her waist and arms round her neck. The adult embraces the child firmly and can spin round with the momentum of the jump. Children who have been supported and contained by their parents are able to cling to adults, but many mentally handicapped children may not know how to cling on and perhaps may not want to. It would be wrong to expect this kind of relationship play until the necessary physical confidence and trust has been established.

It is important that the adult who works with mentally handicapped children is able to take a child's weight with great understanding and care. All the activities of supporting, rocking, swinging, bouncing, containing, climbing and balancing are normally mixed up so that often three types of support occur at once. All the child knows is that the activities are enjoyable and rewarding. The adult has the satisfaction of seeing the child grow in confidence and in his ability to relate to others.

5. Using the floor for support

Experiences using the floor for support give a child greater awareness of his body as a whole as well as of the different parts of his body. The easiest way to help a child enjoy being on the ground is to slide him along, pulling him by his wrists or his ankles. Awareness of the centre of the body and the flexibility of the spine can be developed by swaying the child gently from side to side as he lies on the floor, allowing the waist to 'give' and the arms to swing freely.

Spastic children particularly benefit from being rocked gently from one side to another when they are lying on their backs on the floor. The adult should hold the child firmly and gently by the shoulder and hip and help him to let go of his weight as he falls from his side onto his back. The adult should notice if the child can let his head rest on the floor, and if he is supple or stiff in the centre of his body.

Special care children, who are mentally and physically severely handicapped, enjoy being pulled along on a blanket and being rolled on a soft mat, and I have often seen spasticity decreased as a result of these experiences. An adult can sit back on his heels and roll the child's body so that it lies across his thighs, with the child's stomach pressing down; he can rock the child slightly, patting his back, and then gently let him roll off his thighs back onto the ground again. This kind of rocking impresses on the child that he has a middle.

It is important in this kind of play that the adult–child roles should be reversed so that, if the child is capable of doing so, he can roll the adult over the floor, and several children working together can give the adult a slide. All the types of relationship play described so far are 'with' relationships, but there comes a time when the adult must help the child to develop his strength, if he has not yet done so, or to experience his strength against an adult who helps him to canalise and to focus his energy.

6. Relationships against the adult

Through 'against' relationships an adult can help a mentally handicapped child experience his energy, control his strength and help him to be physically firm and stable. Some children are frail and others are strong and uncontrolled; an adult has to be able to adapt to children with very different needs.

Pushing. An adult can give a child a ride by pushing back to back along the floor; sometimes the child is strong enough to give the adult a ride. The adult can help the child to be strong and stable by helping him to be a 'rock', maintaining his position against careful testing. The child can lie, spread out, on his back or his front, 'sticking' to the floor, and holding on with his hands and arms, feet and legs while his partner apparently tries to move him off his base, but must not succeed in doing so. However, when the child tries to move the adult, he should be allowed to succeed after he has exerted all his strength. Stability and strength can be experienced in a sitting position, the child having his feet apart and his hands and fingers spread out, holding the floor at each side and slightly behind him. In this four-square position he can resist the adult's attempts to move him. Another steady base can be created by kneeling on all fours, with one leg bent out sideways, foot gripping the floor. In the beginning a child is more interested in testing the adult's steadiness than in maintaining his own, but children enjoy mock battles and the adult has the satisfaction of feeding in the experience of strength to the child. The next experience is of standing firmly; this needs a fairly wide base and flexed knees. I have seen mentally handicapped adolescents standing, with hands on each other's shoulders, pushing against each other. They can also push shoulder to shoulder and hip to hip. This is a test of steadiness and determination rather than a contest or demonstration of superior strength. Adolescents can become sensitive in the way they relate their strength to the needs of younger, smaller children.

Pulling. An anxious child will often enjoy tugging against an adult, whereas he finds pushing demands too much involvement with another person. Children like trying to pull an adult up to a standing position. The adult and child, standing, can hold wrists and pull, and again the adult has to know how much strength to exert so that the child is successful in his efforts.

A great deal of the movement education of mentally handicapped children is geared towards developing awareness and control of the knees and developing strength and stability in the legs. In both pulling and pushing strength is directed along a straight line, and these activities are extremely valuable in helping the child direct his energy, focus his strength and concentrate on what he is doing. 'Against' experiences help the child to experience, organise and control his energy, and if the experience is enjoyable and rewarding he is helped to develop a positive relationship to his energy and strength.

Sensitivity and fine touch. A child who is secure in his own strength will be more likely to be able to be gentle and sensitive to others. Most mentally handicapped children enjoy rocking each other to sleep, and they enjoy leading and looking after a partner whose eyes are shut. To be able to close his eyes and be led shows growing self-confidence and indicates that the child is more likely to be 'listening' to and benefiting from inner experiences.

The qualities of gentleness and sensitivity may be developed through movement activities involving care of another person. It is a good idea to finish a relationship play session with an activity which is gentle and caring, although, in the early stages, the quality of care may be rather superficial.

A summary of the aims of relationship play

1. To help a child to relate to adults and to other children through encouraging him to respond and through rewarding him for his efforts.
2. To enable a child to experience the fun, satisfaction, and sense of well-being which comes from movement play with others.
3. To encourage a child to communicate through non-verbal movement play and through using sounds, singing and, eventually, language.
4. To give a child security and confidence, both physical and emotional.

5. To develop a child's awareness of himself through activities with and against adults and other children.
6. To develop the caring aspects of a child's personality so that he experiences involvement with others, sensitivity to others, and responsibility for others.
7. To develop a child's capacity to make decisions, to find solutions to problems and to develop initiative.
8. To help a child to follow one activity with another, to make fluent transitions from one activity to another, and to develop a sequence of activities.
9. Perhaps the most important contribution that relationship play can make to the development of mentally handicapped children is that it can help children to focus attention on what they are doing, and, with practice, their concentration increases. Movement play is rewarding; a child is involved in what he is doing because the activity is appropriate to his stage of development; he experiences success and so he learns to concentrate.

Aspects of relationship play

1. Transactions between adult and child

At first the child receives movement experiences of being supported, contained, rocked, bounced, rolled and swung with no apparent response or reaction. The child may appear unaware of the adult working with him and there may be no eye contact. He passively accepts the sensations of free flow, of being held and tickled, and the sounds of the adult's voice. However, these experiences make him aware that he has a body and that his body is solid and has weight.

The adult provides 100% of the relationship and the child virtually does not respond at all.

After a time the child begins to respond to the movement play by making sounds, looking at the adult, and perhaps by smiling or laughing. He may reach out to touch the adult, and may imitate his movement or the sounds he is making. The adult responds by imitating the child's spontaneous action or voice sound, and feeds it back to the child. This is the beginning of two-way play or reciprocal play. The child enjoys repetition and gains security from evoking a predictable reaction from the adult.

The adult gives about 80% of the relationship, and the child about 20%.

At the next stage the adult offers himself as something to be played with in the ways described earlier. The child uses the adult's body as apparatus and gains security and confidence from being supported and from being contained. He begins to be aware of his body in relation to the adult's body, and begins to initiate play.

The adult can respond in an expected and familiar way, or he can respond in a slightly different way. The child may or may not respond to a new situation. If he is confident he will indicate new ways of playing himself, or he may want to copy what other children round him are doing with their partners. He gains courage and self-confidence through the sensitive reactions of the adult.

The child and adult may reach the point when both are contributing equally to the movement play and it has become a fifty–fifty relationship.

The child is now ready to do something for the adult. The adult encourages the child to take charge and receives directions from him. Children enjoy looking after their teachers and will work together as a group to roll him over the floor and to pull him, often in different directions to start with. This may be the first experience for a class of children to focus on the same 'problem' and co-operate.

The child brings more to the relationships in active terms than the adult.

It is now appropriate for the child to try his strength against a strong adult in a variety of 'against' relationships. The adult must judge the degree of resistance necessary to permit the child to be successful. Pulling and pushing and all mock battles help him to experience his strength and determination against another person. Like puppies and kittens, mentally handicapped children can benefit from rough-and-tumble play with an adult. The elements of play and drama combine in mock battles to give a great deal of pleasure and satisfaction. It is essential for the adult to have a sense of humour, and to enjoy this energetic play.

2. Children begin to relate to other children

Older mentally handicapped children are able to partner younger children if they have had sufficient preparation in relationship play first. Occasional classes which mix older and younger children are valuable for both groups. It is important to keep the movement play close to the floor in the beginning.

In time children can work together in groups. Two can sit on either side of a third child whom they support with their hands and rock from side to side so that he falls towards first one and then the other. Two children can help a third to jump; this requires a lot of co-ordination of effort. Three children can join hands and tie themselves into a knot; they can sit down in their knot, and try to travel together over the floor.

Three can kneel on all fours side by side and carry a fourth lying on their backs. The whole class can work together, tying themselves into a knot and sitting and standing up together. They enjoy making a long tunnel, kneeling on all fours side by side while each one has a turn at crawling through the tunnel. Smaller children can crawl over the tunnel. This type of group work can develop into dramatic play. The children can surround a 'monster', catch it, drag it off, eat it, can make it better, find a house for it, make a fire to keep it warm, feed it and sing it to sleep.

Children with relationship problems

1. Children who make no response

It is difficult for an adult to continue 'giving' to an unresponsive child, particularly if the child is slowly deteriorating. In large institutions where shortage of staff makes individual treatment almost impossible, children will sometimes withdraw into an inner world where they find what solace they can within their own bodies, by sucking a thumb until there is no nail left, or playing with food in the stomach by regurgitating it and swallowing it again, or rocking incessantly. The more a child is left alone the more cut off he becomes and the harder it will be to make contact with him.

The adult has to invade the child's world and begin with movement play appropriate to the level at which the child is functioning. Perseverance is needed in feeding in basic sensory experiences, maintaining and perhaps increasing flexibility of the body and in encouraging even the slightest sign of physical effort. The human voice is very important, particularly if the child is blind or partially sighted. Even Rubella children who suffer from varying degrees of deafness and blindness can be encouraged to move and to make contact with others. Playing in water has been found to be particularly helpful in achieving this.

2. Children who actively avoid relationships

Some disturbed children develop various stratagems for avoiding contact with people. They may run away, climb high, escape into a fantasy world, and will mostly avoid eye contact. Hyperactive children, children with autistic tendencies, and autistic children present us with extremely difficult problems. We ask ourselves why are the children like this? What threatens them? Why are they so emotionally insecure? With skilled help many of these children are able to commit themselves to relationships and they will usually respond to an adult whom they know they can trust. The more difficult these children are to reach the more they need relationship play. Working with them can be extremely exhausting, but enough progress can be made for the teacher to feel rewarded for his efforts.

A child who actively avoids human contact is often torn between a desire to avoid involvement and desire to share in the fun that other children are having. Such a child may accept physical contact under certain conditions. He may allow someone to push him on a swing, and accept support from an adult when bouncing on a trampette. In both these activities fear of human contact seems to be forgotten in the joy of movement. He will also often accept support in water.

Sometimes a child will allow his full weight to be taken by one or two adults for a swing or a slide along the floor or may accept back-to-back contact. He is more likely to accept contact with an adult who is beside him or behind him out of direct line of vision. Such children seem to fear face-to-face confrontation and direct eye contact can upset them, but sometimes a child may accept such contact if the adult's position is lower than his. He may, however, find it easier to work with another child rather than an adult. It may even be necessary to provide a child-sized figure which a disturbed child can hug or even attack before he can express emotions towards another human being.

When they have learned to trust their teacher, disturbed children will relate physically to him and may use him as apparatus and play without feeling threatened.

Children who actively avoid human relationships can be very disturbing in a movement class. They may have to be caught and given a warm hug and swing or rock before being released. In time they may accept a relationship as unthreatening and so allow repetition. I have worked once a week for a term with an extremely hyperactive and disturbed boy and met with success only in the last week.

3. Children who must dominate a relationship

Some children can relate to others only by seeking to dominate, and this has to be accepted initially. Such a child will exploit an adult's willingness and be rough in the way he handles his adult partner; he will 'shoot' his partner in dramatic play. Normally this type of child appears to feel threatened by gentleness or attempts at containment.

I worked with a disturbed and exceptionally strong adolescent from a hospital school. He was confident in pushing me (back to back) when he was winning, but the moment I exerted pressure on him, he collapsed; he could not let himself be overcome, and could not comprehend a give and take. We were able to relate through shared movement play, side by side, with a lot of eye contact.

An adult has to be aware of children's needs and learns through experience the way to respond. Particularly with dominant children it is necessary to keep play humorous; when a child learns to know and trust an adult he will begin to respond to a shared situation.

Other problems

Some children, once they have found a safe place to be contained in, do not want to leave it, show no initiative, and want to be treated as babies. An adult has to decide how much a child needs the security of being contained and cuddled and how much he should be encouraged to take a more active role. On the whole a child's behaviour indicates his emotional state; even normal five-year-old children will sometimes not leave the security of the adult's safe 'house'.

Often one meets a child who cannot become involved with relationship play because he is watching what everyone else is doing and lacks confidence in himself. Such a child will need a great deal of encouragement to value his own efforts.

One occasionally meets a child whose main form of relationship is a hard thump. Experience shows that this behaviour disappears gradually as the child gains confidence in forming relationships. Some children appear to live in a fantasy world and often show little interest in physical activity. These children can often be reached through dramatic play.

A stuffed doll may be used as a patient, or the teacher may pretend to feel ill and appeal to one of these children to act as 'doctor' or 'nurse'. If a teacher can enter into a child's spontaneous dramatic play by taking on a suitable role, he can share in the child's often lonely fantasy. Gradually the child's solitary imaginative play can be extended so that the other children in the class are involved.

Conclusion

During my long experience of working with a great many disturbed mentally handicapped children I have observed that many of the most disturbed children can make remarkable progress through relationship play. Part of the process is watching other children enjoying themselves; this creates a great desire to join in the fun. Sometimes the first signs of willingness to be involved with another person may come through the child's wanting to be swung on a rope or helped to bounce on a trampette, and in water many children accept contact who would refuse it on land.

It is to be hoped that more and more teachers of mentally handicapped children will bring in volunteers from top classes of secondary schools, or student teachers in training, to work, or play, on a one-to-one basis once a week. By recreating the early parent–child play which the handicapped may have missed, or from which they were not able to benefit when they were younger, we can help the handicapped child discover himself and experience a variety of ways of building relationships with others. Those who help in this work often gain as much from the experience as do the handicapped children.

We have to remember that developmentally retarded children need relationship play experience to help confirm them as individuals and to reinforce early learning experiences of awareness of their own bodies and awareness of other people. We are not asking retarded children to regress to babyhood, but we are setting up situations in which they have another chance to develop resources which are essential for them if they are to get the most out of their lives.

3 'To dance with a smile': successful experience through dance

LILIAN GROVES

A fourteen-year-old special school girl, one of a family of eleven, wrote,

> The one I liked best was the lilac fairy, all sweeps and swing. I was dancing by myself and I was dancing with a smile.

'To dance with a smile' is not an unimportant experience for a girl to whom life has not been kind.

Children are in special schools because they cannot cope with mainstream education. Many children are placed in ESN (M) schools who have been a disruptive force in their secondary or junior school. A very high proportion of pupils come from educational priority areas and are members of large families. In one class of sixteen girls, eleven came from families of five or more children and all but two of the group received free dinners. These children begin school with a great many disadvantages. Before very long a pattern of failures, constantly repeated, is established. Individuals respond to failure by withdrawing from or kicking at life.

The beneficial results arising from some experimental dance lessons were reported in Chapter 1. Subjective views are not acceptable in empirical research, but one cannot but feel that if only one child who was 'born to fail' learned what it was to 'dance with a smile', the lessons would have been worth while. Naturally this is not the only justification for dance but it seems to me an important one and the one which I wish to emphasise here.

This chapter gives practical suggestions so that other teachers, who perhaps have not yet tried dance, may see whether their pupils might also have successful experiences. Though the ideas and methods described relate to secondary-age educationally subnormal girls, many of them may be applied to other groups. A great many quotations are used to show 'customer reaction' to dance lessons. Those quoted were all aged thirteen to sixteen years and attended ESN (M) schools. Except where necessary to clarify meaning the original spelling and punctuation have been left.

The form of dance is broadly based upon the teaching of Rudolph Laban, of whose work the majority of teachers have at least an elementary knowledge. Dance is expressive movement used consciously as an art form. Though used initially here for therapeutic ends, the aesthetic nature of dance is not ignored. Dance was once described as 'having many faces', but all forms originally fulfilled the need to communicate ideas or moods, to express a deeply felt emotion. Many types of dance were seen by Laban and others to have become mere forms removed from reality. As Douglas Kennedy, the famous collector of folk dances, put it, 'they have become stilted, white, filleted, insincere'. Modern Educational Dance or Creative Dance was an attempt to return to sincere dance. This form of dance is not restricted to one type of rhythm, spatial pattern, bodily movement or dynamic quality. This is not to say that there is no technique. Teachers who believe dance is simply 'free expression' or 'movement to music' cannot involve their pupils in meaningful experiences. However, it is true to say that this form of dance is concerned with individual expression and enriching personal powers rather than with learning set dances or dance exercises. The unique advantage of this approach is that technique and opportunity for creativity can be given side by side from the earliest lessons.

The basic material of dance

A simple analysis of the basic materials employed in creative dance may be given in terms of body awareness, space awareness, the dynamics of movement and relationships.

Body awareness, or 'What is moving?'

Even if one's movement is limited to one hand it is possible to dance; dance can take place in the hands as well as in the feet. Individual fingers can meet and part; the hand can be folded in to its centre and shoot out wide. Hands can be shaken, can grasp one another, rub against or strike one another. The hands can dance a long way from the body or very close to it; one hand may lead and the other follow, sometimes catching up or overtaking it. The hands can tell stories – the rain is falling, the sea flowing, birds flying, flowers opening. One person's hands may dance with another's, producing a 'dance for four hands' or six or more. Initially it is probably easiest to sit and concentrate all movement into the hands. Later one can develop hand dances bringing more involvement of the rest of the body. A television programme led to one small group obtaining white gloves to create a 'theatrical hand dance', and the use of standing floodlights brought very interesting shadow dances for hands.

Dancing with the feet is obvious, but different sensations arise from dancing on the toes, on flat feet or on moving from toes to heels. Feet can caress the floor or stamp or move scarcely making contact with the floor. Dancing feet can thrust the body into the air. Even these very simple movements can be used creatively and can bring out individual preferences. One girl liked long low steps because it made her feel very peaceful; another enjoyed skimming over the ground making complicated steps 'like embroidery', and many enjoyed leaping and turning in the air because it made them feel 'free' and 'happy'.

Hands and feet may dance at the same time; light stepping movements with quick changes of direction can be accompanied by darting, flicking hand movements.

But dance is not only for hands and feet; elbows and knees can 'appear' and 'disappear'; head and shoulders can dance. One group enjoyed developing isolated movements of head, shoulders and hands in an 'arab' style dance.

Different parts of the body can lead a movement; the elbow may lead in a turning movement; the chest, the centre of 'levity', can lead the body in a flying movement. Different parts of the body can meet, make contact and leave one another. For example the right elbow can make contact with the left knee before exploding away from it to begin a new movement phrase.

Basic body actions include stepping, jumping, turning, gesturing, sliding and rolling. Any one of these or series of these can be built into dance-like phrases.

Body awareness includes awareness of shape. Not only should dancers be aware of completed shapes – usually described as pin, wall, ball and screw – but they should sense the relationship of one part of the body to another; they should feel the difference between a symmetrical shape and one which is asymmetrical.

When we emphasise this aspect of movement we are making children aware of exactly *what* the body is doing. For adolescents this can readily be achieved in the context of dance-like experiences.

Space awareness, or 'Where are you moving?'

The concern here is with floor and air patterns. The feet trace out patterns on the floor and the limbs create air patterns.

Richard Aske, tutor to the young Queen Elizabeth I, said:

> Rising and falling, going out and coming in, advancing and retreating, there are in nature no movements other than these.

Such movements may take place within one's own 'kinesphere', one's own 'personal space'; that area which can be reached without travelling from the spot. Or the focus may be beyond our kinesphere and out into general space, when the movement becomes a 'travelling' dance. Within a simple movement such as rising and falling the 'focus', the 'intention' can create dramatic emphasis. Focusing high and moving from low to high creates a harmonious movement; focusing high and moving from a high position to one which is deep creates considerable tension.

At an earlier stage children become conscious of moving forwards, backwards, sideways, at a high, medium or deep level. These directions relate to the position of the body but interesting 'space' dances can develop by setting such tasks as moving towards and away from two adjacent walls and the ceiling, i.e. focusing on these spots and using different parts of the body to lead the movement, as well as showing different movement qualities.

Important contrasts may be brought about by working on central and peripheral movements, gestures 'near to' and 'far from' the centre of the body. Withdrawn girls tend to enjoy central movements while those more extrovert enjoy the freedom of peripheral movement.

If space awareness is the central theme for a lesson we are helping a child relate the bodily self to its environment. As children develop their own dances they will always be asked to consider *where* they are moving.

Dynamics of movement, or 'How are you moving?'

Here we are concerned with the *quality* of movement. All movement has quality, even if it is only the quality of 'heaviness', but here we have a rich source of material by means of which we can focus on one particular aspect. The dynamics of movement are concerned with attitudes to time, weight, space and flow.

Time. Movements may be quick or slow, they may be sudden or sustained; they may be restless or unhurried. Movement may accelerate or decelerate.

Weight. Movements may involve a great deal of muscular tension and be powerful or firm; they may involve much less tension and be delicate, showing fine touch. If a movement is heavy it involves very little tension; the body simply flops about.

Space. This section is not concerned with *where* we move but *how.* Movement may attack the air round the body; the limbs may cut through space, piercing it; they may indulge in space filling air with movement, taking winding, flexible paths.

Flow. A movement may be freely flowing, giving the sensation of going on and on, or it may be bound, that is capable of being stopped at any moment and having this sensation built in to the movement.

One element cannot be isolated but a beginner's attention can be focused on one aspect. Later the dancer becomes more aware of combinations of movement. The eight basic combinations, known as 'efforts', were described by Laban as follows:

Time	*Weight*	*Space*		*Effort*
Quick	Strong	Direct	=	THRUST
Quick	Strong	Indirect	=	SLASH

Time	*Weight*	*Space*		*Effort*
Quick	Light	Indirect	=	FLICK
Quick	Light	Direct	=	DAB
Slow	Strong	Direct	=	PRESS
Slow	Strong	Indirect	=	WRING
Slow	Light	Indirect	=	FLOAT
Slow	Light	Direct	=	GLIDE

Some teachers use these effort qualities as the basis of their teaching. This approach can be rather sterile if it takes on a drill-like quality but it can be a rich source of creative movement.

Individuals often have personal preference for one type of movement rather than another. The girl quoted in the opening paragraph of this chapter was joining in a dance based on the *Pas de six* from Tchaikovsky's *Sleeping Beauty.* Another girl, regarded by her teachers as extremely aggressive, wrote, 'I liked the fairy with the big jumps. I was stabbing. I was punching and wiping. It made me feel good.' Another, physically rather feeble, wrote, 'I liked the lovy slow music, it was dreemy.' While still another liked 'the one what was all flicks and flutters. I was all trembly and fussy.'

But the dreamy girl learned to leap and the aggressive girl to move with calm measured step.

Relationships, or 'With whom do you dance?'

It is when plenty of opportunity is given for partner and group work that we can hope for improved inter-personal relations. But we must not forget the importance of solo dances. Each individual sometimes needs to move alone, even if alone in a crowd. For children who are normally restless or disturbed in any way solo dancing offers the chance to become really absorbed; it creates much less demand than dance, where one must adapt to the requirements of another. While some girls become worried and confused if introduced too early to partner work, others, particularly more senior beginners, feel 'safer' and less noticeable when working in a group. Others, perhaps more able than the rest, need to dance alone from time to time to extend themselves fully. One girl who had very good bodily control and who showed great sensitivity to music became irritated when her small group did not respond to the music as she thought they should. She wrote in her diary, 'I like doing the witches dance when the group co-operates but most of all what I like doing is when you dance by yorrself because you can do the movement you know is rite.' This girl needed her moments of personal interpretation quite as much as the girls with limited body awareness but she, like them, needed to learn to work in harmony with others.

Several ways of developing partner work have proved successful with older slow learners. Simple couple dances proved popular. These involved ways of approaching and leaving a partner, copying a partner's dance, moving together in unison, making up a duet of question and answer in movement and so on. Very popular was the opportunity to lead and to follow a partner. Sometimes the follower closed her eyes and relied on the leader for safety and enjoyment. Different types of musical accompaniment led to a variety of dance patterns. Some children proved natural leaders as did the one who wrote, 'When we was leading our partners I felt important I reely did.' Others found it difficult to lead but enjoyed being led. A few were afraid to let a partner lead, but after a short time with the teacher leading confidence developed.

Material sometimes helps in the early stages; two girls with a large piece of material 'make the material dance'. The co-ordination required is quite difficult but many girls in my experimental classes enjoyed this, and some advanced to dancing in fours with two pieces of material with which they produced interesting inter-woven patterns. Simple group dances can be developed on the 'follow-the-leader' theme with the leader 'winding' the file into a kind of labyrinth or creating a farandole.

Interesting group dances arise from exploring the special relationships dictated by the number in the group. Trios give rise to particularly dramatic dances. One group of girls towards the end of a six-month dance course enjoyed exploring the possibilities of a trio – two dancers split by one, one torn by two, two surrounding one, three in disharmony and three in harmony. One girl related the basic pattern of one against two to her own life experience and she and her two friends developed a dance which played out the relationship of father, mother and daughter.

All dance lessons involve these ideas of *what*, *where*, *how* and *with whom*, though the weighting will differ from lesson to lesson. Even the simplest ideas will produce creative movement. For example a group may work on ways of rising, falling and spreading using different speeds and tensions. From the exploration an individual will select and refine to produce his own dance. Or a group may find ways of rising, falling and spreading as a group. One child will simply enjoy the action while another will have an image in his mind. Sometimes the teacher presents the class with an image as a stimulus for dance. In this situation the teacher might start with the theme 'fire' and develop movement through consideration of the path of gently spiralling smoke and the direction taken by fiercely leaping flames. Sometimes the image will arise from the movement. A fountain dance arose from group experience of rising and sinking.

Children in special schools or remedial classes need much repetition to become conscious of the essence of an action and yet they may become bored by too frequent repetition. However, as the last paragraph shows, it is possible to evolve many different settings for one basic idea.

Some experts in dance insist that 'imaginative' ideas should not be introduced until children have developed a fairly extensive movement vocabulary. They suggest that if the initial approach is via 'images' or 'stories', dance will be of poor quality and largely meaningless. While I share their distaste for dance based along the lines of 'be a tree', I believe it is possible to give sound movement training and at the same time widen children's experience through the use of poetry, story, music and other stimuli.

It is possible to structure dance lessons so that there is scope for full involvement of every member of the class. There should be no 'right' and 'wrong' in dance, though there will be more and less thoughtful and refined movement. A pupil's typical movement, jerky or lethargic, tight or open should be acceptable, and recognition and acceptance of one's own type of movement can lead to awareness and appreciation of the movement of others. Dance may give children who are unable to concentrate the chance to become really absorbed, and give those who are unable to express themselves in words a different and very personal means of expression. This is probably the kind of successful experience one could expect to transfer to other situations.

Beginning dance with older girls

The commonest question asked by teachers at demonstrations is, 'But how do you get them started?' It is a simple matter to get unselfconscious young children to dance. Dance is a natural and universal means of expression. Unfortunately our culture does not readily encourage bodily expression and adolescent girls are notoriously self-conscious.

One very successful teacher of dance had her slow learners make masks. This seemed to make the girls feel invisible. When they had gained confidence they happily discarded their masks. I often give girls pieces of attractive material, usually chiffon, nylon or silk which they 'cause to dance'. (Initially I begged old head scarves from friends but soon I was haunting market stalls buying pretty-coloured, light and very cheap material by the metre.) In concentrating on the material most girls – though not all – cease to be embarrassed. The use of an uncomplicated and steady rhythm to accompany the movement appears to release emotional, and therefore excessive muscular, tension. Initially some may simply watch the dancing material without much bodily involvement but once confidence is gained it is easy to extend the movement. A few really nervous girls may drape the material over their face. When this happens I try to use it. For example an 'Indian' hand dance, with everyone veiled, has brought even the most reluctant into the lesson. Only in one class was this not 100% effective. In this class there were two very retarded girls who took two weeks to get as far as taking off their shoes and coming into the hall. They then spotted some large pieces of material and each retired under one for the rest of the lesson. The following week they made straight for their cover. Everyone was then asked to get a large piece of material and we worked on a 'ghost' dance to the music of Saturn from Holst's 'Planet Suite'. After a while the reluctant ones were drawn in since they could move without revealing their identity. One of the brighter girls in the class suggested that some of the class should be children who were chased by ghosts. The 'children' worked out a dance which bore some resemblance to the Western Theatre Ballet's *Street Games*. After this the two nervous girls joined in regularly, though one from time to time, whenever she was upset, retired to her private world beneath her special 'cover'. She was left undisturbed until she chose to emerge.

Music or some other form of accompaniment provides another 'safe' framework. On the principle of going from the known to the unknown pop music is sometimes used. It has to be selected with care, however, since only too often the children's response is to jig in the usual thoughtless manner or to giggle with embarrassment at the intrusion of their other life into school. I have found children who have never before listened to anything other than 'pop' (and often they do not really listen to that) become enthralled by quite 'difficult' music. One girl, thirteen years old, said to have an IQ of 60 and scarcely able to read a word, showed tremendous feeling for music and asked many searching questions about it. She developed a particular love for Chopin. Sometimes I have made mistakes in the choice of music. On one occasion when we were working on the theme of a storm at sea I played a favourite piece from Britten's *Peter Grimes*. Afterwards one girl wrote, 'I did not like that first storm music becos it fritn me. It made me hide my head.' Another wrote, 'I did not like that fast nosy music it made me all funy insid.' None was really happy with it and I abandoned it in favour of the more familiar theme from the 'Onedin Line'. The majority of girls reacted most favourably to waltz music. They enjoyed following the simple movement pattern of the music. One girl wrote of a dance to Saint-Saëns' 'The Swan', 'The music is very sweet. I went up and down and round and round as lite like a feather. It made you forget everything nasty.'

Lesson plans

It will already be clear that the teacher of dance must be a very flexible person. The teacher must be ready to learn with and from the pupils and to adapt his plans to suit the reactions and the mood of the class. It is particularly important with the type of children described in this book to accept suggestions from individuals and weave these into the lesson. Though dance itself permits little chance of failure, if the teacher of dance is too rigid in interpreting textbooks on dance or in insisting on his interpretation of a theme or music, then *he* will cause a sense of failure.

However, flexibility, especially in the early stages, must be based on carefully planned lessons. Individual lessons are usually, though not inevitably, structured as follows.

Part 1: Introduction. A simple dance activity to establish the mood of the lesson. A simple dance from a previous lesson may be appropriate.

Part 2: Movement experience. Individual exploration or work in pairs or small groups on the central theme of the lesson.

Part 3: Climax. An individual or group dance using ideas explored in part 2 of the lesson. The dance may be based on an external stimulus or on the movement itself.

The lesson should end with a quiet movement.

Whenever possible I follow dance lessons with a period in the classroom during which the pupils are encouraged (but not forced) to develop ideas or feelings awakened during the lesson. As is already obvious many girls described in this chapter tried to express their reactions in words. Every girl had a dance diary with an attractive cover and with lined and blank pages. Before they began to dance very few of these girls had voluntarily put pen to paper. The names of dances and music were written on the blackboard as were any other words requested, but otherwise the girls wrote what they wished. Some drew in their diaries and others began to paint. With one class the teacher provided large sheets of paper and plenty of paint. Sometimes a group which had danced together created a group painting. Other girls began to model clay and some recorded their reactions on tape.

An example of one lesson (an early lesson with a class of thirteen- and fourteen-year-old ESN (M) girls).

Main themes: Body parts and body shape in stillness. Sudden and sustained movement. Quality in stillness.

Equipment: Music (taped): 'The Swan' (Saint-Saëns' *Carnival of the Animals*); 'Popcorn' (Russ Conway); 'Gnomes' (from Mussorgsky, *Pictures at an Exhibition*); 'Flight of the Bumble Bee' (Rimsky-Korsakov)
Percussion – wooden block, gong
Pieces of material
Piece of twisted wood

Introduction (Aim – to reduce self-consciousness and to develop awareness of musical patterns)
Dance, with material, to the music of 'The Swan'
Instructions. Take a good starting position . . . Show where the first movement is going . . . Look at the material . . . Be quite still . . . At the end of the dance come to a smooth end and be still. (Repeat of dance taken in first and second lessons – the girls were now familiar with music and had discussed the pattern.)

Movement experience 1. Sudden movements – accompaniment: teacher striking wooden block for (*a*) and 'Flight of the Bumble Bee' for (*b*) (*a*) Instructions. Listen to the sound . . . Give yourself a surprise . . . one shoulder, chin, tummy . . . Keep quite still between movements.

(*b*) Instructions. Sit down and listen to the music . . . Let your hands dance all round you as you listen . . . good. This time let your feet take you all over the floor . . . good. Were you really light and very fast? . . . Did you bring in lots of changes of direction? . . . If you listen hard the music tells you when to change . . . Repeat.

2. Sustained movements – accompaniment: teacher using gong

Instructions: Watch your hand . . . Let it go on moving as long as you can hear the sound . . . Don't stop until the sound has quite disappeared . . . When the sound stops be quite still . . . It is a different kind of stillness from that in the sharp dance . . . It still feels as though it is reaching on . . . smooth, long movements . . . Let the movement take you high and low and turn you round.

Climax (Two alternative forms of climax for this lesson)

Alternative 1. 'A Jerky Dance for Three' – music: 'Popcorn'

Instructions: Sit down in threes . . . Listen to the music and let your hands move in time to it . . . What kind of movement? . . . When the music stopped did your hands freeze? . . . Stand up and make an interesting picture in threes . . . Your picture should show what kind of movement you are going to do . . . Share your space and watch one another as you move . . . good . . . When you froze did the whole group make a spiky shape? . . . Would it be better to finish at different levels?

Alternative 2. 'Witches' – music: 'Gnomes'

Instructions. Sit round me and look at this piece of wood . . . Does it make you imagine anything? . . . Can you see the twists in the wood? . . . Listen to this twisty music . . . What other movements does the music suggest? . . . Let your hands move to the music . . . Were you still when there was silence? . . . This is yet another kind of stillness . . . How do you feel when you are still? . . . Stand up and see if you can get your body to twist and stop in strange shapes . . . How do you think the dance ends? . . . Go into groups of two or three and talk about your dance.

The teacher discusses individually with the groups both their dramatic ideas and how they will develop them in movement. The groups work on their dances – they will be further developed in following lessons.

Follow-up work. On returning to the classroom following this dance about witches, some girls wrote about the lesson, some painted, one made a twisted model witch from a wire coat-hanger with the help of the teacher and some recorded their impressions on tape. 'The witch one was good. I like the music it is exciting. The wood looked like an elephant in pain. It looks like a little old man. The music was all twisted with stops. You didn't know at first when it was going to stop. I got myself into a twisty shape and when the music stopped I was in a spiky shape. We pretended we made a spell up. I didn't always like the stopping bits. I felt like going on and on. At the end we all ran away into the woods.'

Examples of dances built up over several weeks

Dances based on stories from various sources

1. Sleeping Beauty. I have several times referred to this dance. Its inspiration came from a visit to the theatre to see the Royal Ballet. The girls were full of their visit. The following dance was built up over five weeks and the girls decided to make 'props' and costumes so that they could dress up and give a performance when it was completed. Costumes were simply pieces of material draped or pinned but head-dresses and garlands were made.

Scene 1: 'The Christening'

(*a*) Court procession – music: 'The Grass is Green' from BBC recording of the sound-track of *Elizabeth R*
(Music selected because a girl suggested having a dance 'like the ones on telly')
Movements – floor patterns and sustained movements
The group enjoyed learning a very simple step and floor pattern created by the teacher

(*b*) The rocking dance – music: Elgar's 'Chanson de Matin'
Movements – sustained movement and mirror work in twos

(*c*) The six good fairies – music: *Pas de six* from Tchaikovsky's *Sleeping Beauty*
Movements – thrust, slash, glide, float, flick and dab

(*d*) Wicked fairy and the curse – music: *Sleeping Beauty*
Movements – thrust, slash, wring and dab
The soloist described her dance in a tape recording:
'I like making up new dances especially with other girls but the best dance of all is the wicked fairy dance where I leap in the air. I wear a long black cloak. It flies out behind me like wings. I stab and I wring. I have to frighten them all but the best part is the start when I leap from the table.'

Scene 2: In the garden, sixteen years later

(*a*) The garland dance of the princess and friends – music: 'Sleeping Beauty Waltz'

Movements– floor patterns and relationships

(*b*) The prick – after much trial and error we decided to use percussion (wire scraper on a drum; handle strikes rim for actual 'prick') for this section, which was largely mime

(*c*) The forest grows up – music: Grieg's 'Morning Mood' (from *Peer Gynt*)
Movements – rising and spreading with sustainment

(*d*) The arrival of the prince – music: Grieg's 'Norwegian Wedding Dance' (from 'Norwegian Dances')
Movements – Step and floor pattern

(*e*) The court awakes – processional dance repeated

2. *The Creation Story.* The Bible is a wonderful source of inspiration for dance. This one was performed for the school assembly.

(*a*) Nothingness – 'void' – music: 'Echoi' (Foss, *The Fragments of Archilochos: Non-Improvisation*)
Movements – heavy, aimless, contrasting with sharp rushes – confusion

(*b*) Light – music: Grieg's 'Morning Mood'
Movements – rising and spreading with gliding

(*c*) Land – music: 'Architecture' from John Dalby's 'Pageant of Dances'
Movements – changing shapes – group shape – pressing

(*d*) Waters – music: Debussy's 'Poisson d'Or'
Movements – floor patterns in groups – dabbing and flicking

(*e*) Plants – percussion: scrapers and shakers
Movements – growing and spreading with variety of shapes

(*f*) People – Vaughan-Williams' 'Sons of the Morning', from *Job*
Movements – body awareness, gliding, relationships

Dances based on poetry

There are several useful collections. Particularly good are Stokes' *Word Pictures as a Stimulus for Creative Dance*, Baldwin and Whitehead's *That Way and This*. For example, 'The Shadow' by Stokes developed into 'Echoes', to the music of 'Tokyo Melody' (the BBC signature tune for the Tokyo Olympics). This was a demanding dance requiring from 'the echo' an exact copy of gestures and steps but using less tension than the original.

Dances based on the weather

Snow.

(*a*) Snow fall – music: Debussy's 'The Snow is Falling', from *Children's Corner*
'It started smooth and slowly; that was like snow flakes. You made your

hands all curvey. Sometimes you twirl and whirl fast. At the end you are gently on the floor. You make nice patterns in the dance.'

(*b*) The frost – music: Vivaldi's 'Winter' from the *Four Seasons*

'I like the sharp movements like the frost. It was like being very cold. You move with your hands and feet and legs and fingers all stiff. You have to keep making shapes like statues.'

(*c*) Children playing – music: Quilter's 'Children's Overture'

'We made a dance out of movements like throwing snowballs and rolling big snowballs and jumping into piles of snow and making footsteps in the snow. You didn't just act, you danced.'

(*d*) The skaters – music: Meyerbeer's 'Skaters' Waltz'

'The skating was fun. We started off with an expert then some more came and fell down then we joined in and skated with a step hop hop and we all made lovely patterns.'

Dances based on visual and tactile experiences

Two-dimensional patterns and three-dimensional shapes from sculpture or from nature may spark off dance. Through the use of such materials children are led to look with more discernment at the world around them. Sometimes the pupils may paint pictures which may then be translated into 'plastic' shapes in dance. The teacher may produce a design using curved, angular, twisted and linear pathways; by the use of thin and thick lines the amount of tension may be suggested; by the use of dots and gaps jumps may be indicated. On one occasion following the use of the music of the 'gnomes' described above the teacher produced a design inspired for her by that music. Surprisingly one girl recognised the movement she had danced the previous week. One way of introducing spatial designs which I found helpful with a group of rather maladjusted girls was by the use of ribbons. One particularly difficult member of that group missed the first four lessons and came reluctantly to the fifth. At the end of the lesson she wrote (with frequent reference to the teacher for spellings):

I lik the ribon dans be cos we had five perple and we mad a patin in the sky. We did sum nice patins and shapes we did curve shapes and wavey shapes and the ribbon did loop and twirl and you fly round the room and it was lovely. There was red blue purple green yellow pink ribons and they was made of silk and when the dans finish we made a lovely still picture it was good you bend down and up and you twist around and you go fast and slow. I had a pink ribon and I lik jigging the ribbon in the sky.

The use of a piece of driftwood to help children to think about shape has already been mentioned. Other natural objects such as stones and shells can be brought in, or the class may be taken to look at trees in the school ground or at patterns in the clouds.

Handling materials brings another dimension to the experience. The smoothness of a stone, the full richness of velvet, the roughness of a pan scrubber, the softness and strange lack of resilience of polystyrene can all play a part in increasing awareness and in giving inspiration for dance.

Dances based on the shape of or story behind a piece of music

Some reference has already been made to this type of dance. Two further illustrations may help.

The music from the film *Zorba the Greek* offers many ideas. 'Zorba's Dance' lends itself particularly to the exploration of relationships from moving alone – discovering oneself – to meeting one other and discovering the possibility of relationships in twos, then in fours and into a large group. The music ends with a return to the starting-point, with the individual withdrawing into himself.

Music which tells a story is not always easy to use. Often the most interesting pieces are too long for even experienced dancers in school. Perhaps the most successful are those which are made up of several short pieces but can be woven into a whole. Saint-Saëns' *Carnival of the Animals* is one such piece. Mussorgsky's *Pictures at an Exhibition* is full of gems. Dances based on ballets or part of them often prove popular with girls who secretly, and sometimes openly, see themselves as ballerinas.

A child describes a dance based on Rossini–Respighi's *La Boutique Fantasque*:

> We pretended to be toys in a shop. The manager wound us up to show us off to customers. When the manager went home he left a boy in charge. The boy started to dust then he wound them up and we all started to move. Some was Can-Can dolls, some was bride dolls. We all went round the shop with different movements. When we wouldn't stop the boy didn't know what to do and the dolls fell down. The manager was angry and ran after the boy. It was good. I was a Spanish doll and I spin round with my tambourine and I was all lite and happy.

Again and again the girls used the words 'I felt happy', 'I was happy', 'I felt beautiful', 'I felt good'. Could there be a better recommendation for the use of dance with children who so often appear at odds with life?

To emphasise this point I want to end with a few case studies. Hazel was a very disturbed individual. A year before the dance programme was instituted she had been excluded from a comprehensive school with the description 'behaviour manic'. She was the product of a broken home and lived with her grandmother. The special school report said: 'Fights with her teachers. Epileptic. Hyperkinetic.' Hazel was one of the brightest girls in the group and could express herself well. Of her first dance lesson she wrote,

> I liked all the things we done today. We had a dance it was romantic all my mind was floating on air. Ann talked to us on the tape. She said did we like it we said yes indeed it was like as if you were by yourself in the world it was great.

From time to time in the lessons she was distracted but she never opted out for the whole period. Her behaviour showed steady improvement though she continued to be easily upset and could then be very destructive; this never happened in a dance lesson, however. If Hazel came to the lesson very upset a slow quiet dance with material appeared to soothe her and she behaved well for the rest of the day.

By the third term her teacher reported that outbursts were becoming less frequent. She was increasingly accepted by the rest of the class and her delight in this is shown in this passage:

> Today we did a dance about a ship wreck from a story from the bible. I was captain of the ship. The others said I could be in charge. It was great. We was shipwrecked and I helped get some of the others out. I wish we could dance every day.

Penny had a twin sister and an elder sister in the same special school. They came from a large family and lived in the poorest area of the city. In the first sociometric test Penny was unchosen by her classmates. By the end of the dance programme her popularity had increased and she rated sixth in status. Penny was known for her quick temper and was inclined to hit out at everyone and everything. She had a poor attendance record and the teacher confided that she was relieved when she did not attend. She appeared for the first dance lesson and then did not reappear for the next four. By the time she appeared the rest of the class was enjoying dance. She was ignored and even when asked no one would accept her as partner. The teacher attempted to bring her into the dance but she withdrew to a corner. Eventually she agreed to help accompany the dancers with percussion – temple bells. This appealed to her, and when the rest of the group began to play and dance Penny began to move to her own instrument, though only in her corner. The next lesson she agreed to join in a hand dance and was gradually drawn into the group. As her movement improved so did her behaviour. By the end of the term Penny showed the most improvement in the group in quality of movement and in sensitivity to others. Her awareness of space remained rather poor and she preferred to dance in a limited area. However, she joined in group planning and there were plenty of girls willing to partner her. Her attendance improved and she seldom missed a dance lesson.

Finally, a girl who was very different from Hazel and Penny. Sylvia had a stated IQ of 69 and was an epileptic. Her class teacher wrote of her, 'She often wilts and this has an effect upon both her physical and mental performance.' However the school medical officer said she should take part in physical education lessons.

Sylvia had only one close friend, a girl of very low intelligence. These two chose one another in the sociometric test but were otherwise unchosen. In the behaviour test she scored high on restlessness and unforthcomingness, but low on aggression. During the first dance lesson Sylvia fainted and caused a mild diversion. In the second lesson Sylvia drooped; she gazed into space and appeared unmoved by what went on. In the third lesson she was given a piece of material which she particularly liked. She joined in the 'Indian' dance with the material draped over her head. For the first time she had something to write when she returned to the classroom: 'Sylvia licks the music and dansing and I like dansing with me hands.'

She also joined in a partner dance with her special friend. From then on she took a full part in every lesson. She began to enjoy strong flexible movement; her spatial awareness improved and she moved easily at different levels and directions. Something of her new independence was shown when after a dance on 'the sea' she returned to the classroom and immediately got out the necessary equipment to produce a sea painting. After the first two lessons Sylvia never fainted in a dance lesson and the number of attacks in school greatly diminished. Indeed Sylvia became a changed person; her improved self-image is indicated in her statement, 'When I dance I feel bootiful.'

To feel 'bootiful', to dance 'with a smile' – these experiences, and others which could not be put into words by the dancers, are the reasons why I believe dance has a very important part to play in the education of young people who so frequently experience failure.

4 Competition for physically handicapped children

VEIDA BARCLAY

A child suffering from a right hemiplegia (see p. 52) was admitted to her local primary school. She learned to swim at the near-by Physical Education College and her wise class teacher saw that she joined in as much of the physical education programmes as she was able. With much determined practice she won a place as shooter on the school netball team. She worked hard in school and was popular with other children. Unhappily when she transferred to the secondary school she was considered too handicapped to take part in any aspect of physical education. The effect of this exclusion was startling. From being a friendly, hard-working girl she became so disruptive that she was suspended from school for three months. Admission to an understanding special school helped her to readjust and she became, once again, a happy, well-liked pupil, very involved in physical activity.

Obviously, teachers without special training in work with handicapped children are reluctant to risk possible injury to these 'special' pupils and are perhaps uninformed about the value of games and athletics to physically handicapped children. Equally, teachers working in special schools may have insufficient experience of physical education to attempt a very full programme. This chapter seeks to give both groups practical help.

Physical education and its near relation, sport, embrace a wealth of activities which can be adapted successfully to form a valuable part of the rehabilitation of the injured and the education of the physically handicapped. All that is said in this chapter is intended to refer to both groups. Games and athletics are especially helpful for the wheelchair bound in helping to alleviate weight problems, improve circulo-respiratory efficiency and promote a feeling of well-being. Most important of all, perhaps, is the manner in which participation in some form of sport gives a disabled child or adolescent a degree of independence and a feeling of belonging to the world of young people.

The teacher concerned with physical education is a member of a team, a link in a long chain, and the amount of help and advice available to him will vary from school to school. Certainly the decision to involve a handicapped child in physical education must be taken only with the agreement of the head-teacher, but occasionally he may have to be prodded to seek further support. The school medical officer must be involved in the decision, as must parents. Physiotherapists who have previously treated the child are usually most willing to advise. Support for a teacher is relatively easy to obtain in a special school because there is ready access to medical advice, but where handicapped children are integrated into ordinary schools there is more of a problem.

In future the physical education teacher may well be a member of the assessment team concerned with the full development of 'special' children. This will help to make recommendations such as the following more realistic. 'This child may take light exercise' is a common prescription. What is 'light exercise'? What is its purpose? Is the child lacking in co-ordination? Has he problems of balance, perception, or difficulties in position and spatial relationships? If a child's problem lies in motor organisation, a movement may be broken down into parts, each taught separately, and then the whole performed. Not all teachers agree with this approach but I have found it very helpful. However, the most important point to remember is that each child is an individual; when the most immediate problems have been identified and discussed, one must find the best approach for that individual.

It is important that a teacher working with handicapped children should be conversant with the developmental progress of 'normal' children. Handicapped children develop in much the same way but their development will lag behind those of the same chronological age.

Safety precautions for all handicapped children

All teachers must be safety conscious, but there are many additional precautions which teachers of handicapped children must keep in mind.

Many children are unsteady on their feet and easily fall; attention should be given to the various ways of meeting the floor. In most schools, experience in landing and rolling is gained in the movement lesson.

Ferrules on the bottom of aids such as sticks and crutches should be checked as these wear through very quickly when the child is active, causing the aid to slip.

Floors should be splinter-proof, for often games are played in a sitting position. On grass stones are a hazard. Playing areas should be well away from traffic and footpaths; it is so easy in the heat of a game to run or slide out of play just as someone is passing. A tennis court is an ideal playing area; its enclosure and hard surface facilitate the use of wheelchairs.

It is not within the scope of this book to supply details of all the various conditions a teacher may meet, but particular reference is made here to those handicaps which require specific precautions in some games and athletic activities. Teachers seeking more detail should refer to the bibliography at the end of the book (see also Chapter 7).

Spina bifida. This is a congenital condition consisting of an incomplete development of the roof of the neural arch of one or more of the vertebrae. The lumbar vertebrae are most usually affected but this condition may occur at any level of the spine. The disablement varies with the type and severity of the malformation. It may result in complete or partial paraplegia with loss of bladder and bowel control. In other cases there is normal movement and the condition may be undiagnosed unless the child is x-rayed. There may also be deformities of the feet and hips and this may necessitate many operations and months and even years in hospital. However, more and more spina bifida children are found in normal schools. Some children may take a very full part in a PE programme. Others may receive only medically supervised physiotherapy. Where participation is permitted, there are several special safety precautions to bear in mind. The full or partial *paraplegic* spina bifida child will lack sensation; care must therefore be taken to avoid friction burns caused by sliding on the floor or on ropes. Circulation is poor and blisters and grazes take a long time to heal. These children bruise easily and should not be subjected to pressure on any one part of the body for long periods of time (e.g. they should not play games in a sitting position for a whole lesson). Because legs may easily fracture one must watch children very carefully and teach them to avoid scraping their feet or banging their legs on the floor or against apparatus.

Four out of every five spina bifida babies have *hydrocephalus complications* (commonly referred to as 'water on the brain'). This is a condition where there is a blockage of cerebro-spinal fluid in the brain, and if this is not relieved pressure builds up and the brain may be damaged. Normally an operation is performed on babies which involves inserting a valve behind the right ear (the valve is named after Holter, who devised the operation). The valve opens automatically when pressure builds up and so the excess fluid drains away. The first operation in England was carried out in 1958 and approximately 1,000 operations are now carried out each year. Sometimes the valve may block, and the child then becomes sleepy, has a vague look, feels sick or has a headache; the valve must be checked and medical advice should at once be sought. A child with this condition should not be rushed; the head, if enlarged, is heavy and difficult to control. If quick movements are performed before head control is achieved the head comes out of line and the child may easily lose his balance.

Many spina bifida children have *urinary problems* and wear a urinary bag. By the end of the junior school the majority are toilet-trained, but accidents can happen, especially during a hectic game. A spare pair of shorts should be available. It is also advisable to have somewhere for children who wear this appliance to change, e.g. the medical room; they can be very sensitive about changing in a general cloakroom. Schools adapted to care for the handicapped usually have a room available for changing and in the majority of schools there are specially appointed assistants responsible for the handicapped children. They help the children to arrive on time by assisting them to change quickly. If auxiliaries are not available, older pupils, such as those involved in the service section of the Duke of Edinburgh award scheme, may help.

Many handicapped children in the past have been unable to take part in physical activities because they are too slow at changing and therefore hold up the rest of the class. Whatever assistance is given, however, should aim at helping the child achieve independence.

Care of the *feet* is all important; if socks are worn on perspiring feet and there is a ruck in the sock a blister may result. It is advisable to have talcum powder available, but beware of the child who has an allergy to such powder.

Cerebral palsy. Cerebral palsy is a medical term covering a whole group of neurological conditions involving damage of the motor control centres of the brain, either before or during birth, or at any time later in life. The physical manifestations vary from slight disability at one end of the continuum, to total inability to control movement at the other.

There are three main types of cerebral palsy: spastic, athetoid and ataxic – each type depending on the area of the brain affected. *Spasticity* is the most common type of cerebral palsy. The antigravity muscles are greatly affected by this condition and therefore posture is difficult to maintain. The typical gait of the spastic child is due to tight adductors of the hips, flexed hips and knees and plantar flexion of the ankle, which causes the child to walk on the balls of the feet. If the arms are also involved the elbows are bent and the wrists and fingers flexed. Surgery can help a great deal but the child spends much time in hospital.

Athetosis is the second most common form of cerebral palsy. With this condition the child is unable to control his movement. A voluntary movement in one part of the body leads to unwanted movement elsewhere. Often emotional disturbance makes control worse. Children who are *ataxic* have suffered damage to the cerebellum and have little control, their balance is poor, they are incoordinate and lack kinaesthetic awareness. They therefore have much difficulty in walking.

The condition can also be classified according to the part of the body involved:

Monoplegia (one limb);
Paraplegia (both legs);
Quadriplegia (all four limbs);
Diplegia (four limbs, but the legs much more than the arms);
Hemiplegia (the arm and leg on the same side of the body)

Often the damage extends to other parts of the brain; the child may be affected mentally, may have difficulty in speech and communication or eating, or sight and hearing may be impaired.

The cerebral-palsied child is by far the most difficult to deal with in the ordinary school, but with patience many can achieve a good deal physically.

Special considerations

The congenitally brain-damaged child will have no picture of normality. All normal movements have to be explained thoroughly and taught as a skill breaking them down into component parts. (O. Foreshaw, *PEA* booklet, 1975)

A child injured in this way in later childhood will be confused and, depending on the severity of his injury, will have learning difficulties to a greater or lesser degree, but some memory of 'normality' may return and should be utilised as far as possible.

In all cases it is very important to find something the child can do well. Riding and swimming, dealt with in chapters 5 and 6, are particularly valuable.

In the normal school the less severely brain-damaged child can often hold his own in games; some may even gain a place in a school team. As mentioned at the start of this chapter, even a hemiplegic child may become shooter in a netball team, but if these children are put under too much stress, fatigue may set in and spasticity increase. High-level competition for many is therefore inadvisable.

One should consider the following:

1. Grasp and release is difficult for brain-damaged children; special balls which have ridges are easier to hold and release than small balls. Beanbags are easier to catch because they do not bounce away. Soft, medium-sized balls also facilitate catching.
2. Moving objects are difficult to deal with; it will help to remember that it is
   (*a*) easier to catch a bounced rather than a thrown ball;
   (*b*) easier to kick a stationary rather than a moving ball;
   (*c*) easier to practise hitting a ball (first with the hand and then with an implement) if it is attached by a string to a beam so that it is at exactly the right height.
3. A fast-flying ball may be too difficult to contact, so games such as volleyball must be played with a light ball or a balloon.
4. The ataxic child has difficulty in balance; he should stabilise the body and then move only one part, e.g. be stationary and have a fairly wide base before attempting to throw.

The minimal brain-damaged child (often referred to as the 'Clumsy Child') will be found in all our schools. Surveys conducted in the nineteen sixties amongst children in Cambridgeshire and the Isle of Wight showed that between 6% and 7% suffered from clinically recognisable 'clumsiness' and that most of these children were unrecognised as 'handicapped' by their teachers. The plight of such children is described in Chapter 1. Here it is important to say what teachers should look out for. Watch for the child who has difficulty in tying his shoelaces, buttoning his shirt, who runs awkwardly or trips over his own feet. Watch for the child who always misses the ball. The problem may be poor hand–eye co-ordination, the inability to monitor distance and poor spatial awareness. If a child is noticeably clumsy then he should be referred to the medical officer for tests. Meanwhile he could wear clothes without laces and buttons, and special attention should be paid to him in the general games training programme.

Epilepsy. An epileptic attack is due to an occasional sudden abnormal electrical discharge from part of the brain (about one in two hundred people have this abnormality). There are many different types of fits but the two most generally known are:

1. *Petit mal*, or the small fits ('absences'); this lasts a very short time, the child appearing to be day-dreaming. The child may have several of these fits in a day. Watch for the child who does not seem to be concentrating and do not assume that he simply 'is not paying attention'.
2. *Grand mal*, or convulsive fits; the child may be irritable, feel ill or have a headache prior to the fit. Many speak of this as the 'aura'. During the fit or 'ictus' the child falls to the ground with a cry; there is jerking of the limbs and body; he may froth at the mouth and his face may become blue. Unconsciousness may last up to ten minutes. When the jerking stops there is heavy breathing. After the fit the child is confused for quite some time and he should be allowed to sleep.

It is essential that the epileptic child is accepted by his peers. The disorder is more socially than physically handicapping and the epileptic may be withdrawn for fear of rejection by his schoolfellows. If he does have a fit, help his classmates to understand his difficulties and show them how they can help. As soon as the epileptic falls and the jerking stops, turn him onto his side so that the air passages are free; loosen tight clothing round the neck and keep him quiet until he comes round. Send for help but do not leave the patient. When children understand what is happening even juniors are usually very sensible and cope well. This condition is well controlled by drugs, so make sure the child has taken his medicine.

The epileptic may take part in practically all games and athletic events, but overexcitement should be avoided. Special conditions apply to cross-country running. The epileptic should take part only if there is always someone responsible near at hand, should help be needed, and if the course does not include mountainous terrain or water jumps and is not near a major road. Water is a real hazard to the epileptic, for during a fit he can drown rapidly.

Fits should always be reported. The British Epileptic Association will give advice and information.

Poliomyelitis. This is an infectious disease which used to leave sufferers with a variety of deformities ranging from almost total to minimal paralysis. Fortunately the advent of anti-polio vaccines has virtually wiped out the disease and there can be very few polio victims of school age today. Those who are in school are likely to be able to participate in most of the activities described in this chapter.

Bronchial asthma. When an asthmatic attack occurs, mucus fills the bronchial tubes and the person finds it difficult to breathe. Attacks vary in intensity and the most seriously affected children are likely to be in special schools. For all such children, whether in special or normal schools, physical activity plays an important part in their development. They may play all the individual games described in this chapter; it is important for their future recreation that they develop basic skills. Care should be taken that an attack is not precipitated by too vigorous play or by cold, and the pupil must not be subject to pressure; but at the same time he must be included in as many activities as possible in order that he may feel an accepted part of the group. This requires skilful organisation.

Still's disease. This is a type of rheumatoid arthritis which attacks young children. There is considerable disagreement amongst experts as to its cause. It is sufficient here to say that children suffering from the disease have stiff and painful joints. However, the degree of distress varies from day to day and when they are well they are able to join in many of the activities described in this chapter. Individual activities such as archery, tennis and miniature golf are among the most popular. If there is pain or the pupil appears overtired, he should rest.

Amputation and thalidomide victims. Whether a child is born with a missing limb or limbs or has lost a limb as a result of an accident he will probably have been fitted with an appropriate prosthesis or artificial aid. It is impossible to generalise about what such children can achieve but they must be encouraged to take part in as many physical activities as possible, especially those with value for future adult life. Teachers need to be imaginative in adapting activities to suit individual needs. If a child is unable to use his arms he can play volleyball by heading; ways can be found to attach a table tennis bat to an artificial arm. Many more adaptations than can be given here are possible.

Games

Every physical education programme includes games of some description; they have great value carrying over into adult life. Before considering individual games it is useful to consider the fundamentals common to all games. These are, broadly speaking, footwork and body control, ball-handling and playing within a rule-governed competitive situation.

1. Footwork and body control

Most games require the ability to move on the feet, on the floor or in a wheelchair. It is essential to find some way for the handicapped child to be mobile, and much research is being carried out on mobility aids for the disabled. In order to play games such as basketball, volleyball and deck tennis a child must learn to travel in different directions within a small space. In the early stages, games such as 'Here', 'There' and 'Where' are useful – the children move towards the teacher on the command 'Here', and away from him on 'There' and backwards on the command 'Where'. Practice in changing direction from forwards to backwards and – especially for wheelchair players – in pivoting is important. Various forms of 'tag' and 'dodge and mark' may be played matching partners by ability, e.g. both in wheelchairs. Similarly, games which encourage changes of speed and the ability to stop and start quickly should be taught.

Children in wheelchairs quickly become adept at tipping the weight onto the back wheels of the chair to spin round or even to balance on the spot. Those on crutches or moving with a stick will have to learn to keep their weight over both their feet and these supports and to change direction by putting one foot forwards and then pivoting away from it.

2. Ball-handling

The basic skills are *receiving* a ball, *propelling* it away or *moving with* it.

(*a*) *Receiving a ball.* The ball may be received along the ground or through the air and the receiver may sit or stand. Initially it is easiest to receive from one's own throw; children can work out many ways of throwing and catching on the spot, on the move, with two hands or one, sometimes spinning to catch, sometimes catching a bounce from the floor or a rebound from a wall.

When the child is working with a partner, the ball can be rolled from one to the other (those in wheelchairs fielding and rolling at the side of the chair). One child may chase after a rolling ball, as does a fielder in cricket, overtake it, collect and return it. Children readily move on to throwing and catching in twos, and it is important perhaps to emphasise again the need to match partners according to ability. The more able can then move on to receiving a ball while moving. Children who move with the aid of a stick probably find it easier to receive (and propel) with the feet rather than the hands, and this should be encouraged.

(*b*) *Propelling a ball away.* The ball may be thrown, kicked or hit with the hands or an instrument. Children should be encouraged to be at right angles to the line of propulsion except for chest passes, when the player faces forward. Wheelchairs, where possible, should have the sides removed to allow greater mobility. (There are some chairs especially designed for use in playing games.)

Successful participation in most games requires skill in aiming, and there should be plenty of practice involving aiming at skittles, at targets on a wall, on the floor, into a basket, through a ring and so on. Children should be encouraged to explore ways of propelling the ball with the head and feet as well as hands, to use bats of various sizes and shapes and to aim with quoits and bean-bags as well as balls.

(*c*) *Moving with the ball.* Some games require the player to move with the ball by 'dribbling', as in all versions of hockey and basketball, or occasionally by carrying, as in lacrosse. The former skill will be most commonly required and is frequently included in skill circuits (see p. 76) and in simple races. In its simplest form it develops from 'pat-bouncing', and as skill grows the players should be encouraged to keep their heads up and watch where they are going.

3. Playing the game

A game is a rule-governed competitive activity and children must understand the rules. In the early stages they should be encouraged to decide rules for themselves. For example, children may be given a ball and a net and told to pass the ball across the net. Gradually they will introduce rules to make the game more interesting. Experience in co-operating and outwitting others must be built up gradually in small side games; the teacher can invent ways of developing these skills.

The skill of umpiring a game also needs developing; a severely handicapped child who is unable to join in a team game can find a place as umpire or scorer.

Organising the games lesson

While every teacher develops his own method of organising a lesson, the following points may help non-specialist teachers and students, particularly those taking a group for the first time.

1. Find out in advance the number and ages of players who will be present and the types of disabilities and abilities within the class.
2. Have the apparatus ready before the lesson begins and plan the lesson round the apparatus available.
3. Where appropriate, have permanent floor markings or chalk them in before the lesson begins.
4. Make sure that the floor surface is suitable for the games you have in mind and that there are no 'danger areas'.
5. Make sure children are suitably dressed. Movements may be slow and muscles are more prone to injury when cold.
6. Use your whistle as little as possible, especially indoors. However, children must learn to stop immediately they hear the whistle.
7. Typically a games lesson is divided into a warming-up activity (such as tag), skill training where skills related to the games to be played are learned and practised, and the game or games themselves. However, teachers need not adhere to this plan but should remember that most skills need to be taught and are not simply 'picked up'.

Classification of games according to suitability for the handicapped

Section 1: Individual games or sports. These are particularly satisfying for the severely disabled and for the individualists in the school. They include riding, archery, clock golf and croquet. Such activities may well be continued after schooldays are over.

Section 2: Non-contact games. These include 'net' games such as volleyball, deck tennis and tennis, and field games of the rounders and cricket type. These are useful in that they may be played with relatively little movement; a very handicapped child can have someone act as a 'runner' or to push his wheelchair if he wishes to score a 'run' or travel from base to base in rounders.

Section 3; Contact games. These involve much movement and include hockey and wheelchair hockey, basketball and wheelchair basketball. Some children need the speed and excitement of such games. It is difficult to mix wheelchair players with others and if one can acquire old wheelchairs for more able-bodied players this should be done.

A nervous child should not be forced into competition until he is ready for it, or accidents may occur. Again, the job of umpire may satisfy such a child.

Suggestions for games

The following games have all been used with children and young people with a variety of disabilities and abilities. Some are informal games and some are national games; for these latter the reader is left to look up rules in the official rule book.

1. Individual games

These games may be played by children with a great variety of disabilities; those in wheelchairs may hold their own with the able-bodied. There are two general precautions which apply to all games in this section:

1. Those on sticks or crutches should not stand for too long a period with an injured limb hanging down.
2. Adequate rest should be taken between each game.

This group of games includes bowls, clock golf, miniature golf, croquet and the French game of boules, billiards, darts, skittles, shuffleboard and archery.

Bowls

Bowls is a very popular game. It can be continued as a leisure-time activity; now that ramps are available for the wheelchair patient, the green need not be spoiled. These ramps are easily folded so that they may be carried by car. Many local authority sports centres have greens which allow the use of a wheelchair, and increasingly bowls clubs are opening their doors to 'wheelchair members'. More pressure, however, needs to be brought to bear upon authorities to increase such facilities. A very disabled player can bowl to a partner; this will avoid the necessity of walking the length of the green. The game itself should be of short duration so that those players who are standing will not be overtired. Bowls tournaments add interest, especially if the better players can be drawn to partner the less able.

Croquet

This game is gaining in popularity and may be played by most children and young people. Sets are readily available and include instructions.

Clock golf and miniature golf

Both games are very popular. A miniature golf course may be adapted according to the physical and playing ability of the participants. For those needing support a small flat course is suggested, whilst the more able need the greater challenge of an undulating course. A variety of small golf-type games to play indoors may be developed.

Boules

This is a game played extensively on the Continent; it may be played on any fairly flat piece of ground approximately fourteen metres in length. It is an excellent game for wheelchair and cerebral-palsied players, for they can hold their own in it with the able-bodied. The movements required to play are simple and repetitive.

Apparatus. Continental players normally use a set made of metal, but those most commonly used by holiday-makers are plastic and much lighter and, therefore, more suitable for handicapped players. A set consists of a small (target) ball and eight others.

Marking. A line for the players to stand behind and markers six metres and twelve metres from the line are required.

The game. Players may play on a one-to-one basis with each player having four balls; or they may play in two teams of two with two balls each, or even four teams of four players with one ball each.

The first player, standing behind the delivery line, holds the small ball, palm facing the ground and the back of the hand facing the line of play. The small ball is thrown so that it lands between the six- and twelve-metre markers; he then aims to place his own ball(s) as near as possible to the target ball. The next player tries to do the same thing and, if he is an opponent, he may knock the other's ball further away if he can.

Scoring. Normally players score one point for each ball nearer to the target ball than his opponent. The team add all their scores together. In competition, each set consists of either eleven or fifteen points, and three sets form a game.

There is considerable skill in this game; the fingers may be used to spin the ball as it is released. It has the great advantage that a player can obtain a great deal of pleasure practising on his own.

Shuffleboard

Apparatus. This is an adaptation of the popular deck game played aboard cruise ships. Here the 'cues' are adaptations of oars and these are used to propel flat discs. A very useful adaptation can be made by using lightweight shinty sticks for cues and, if flat round discs are not readily available, a quoit will serve.

Marking. The length of court can be adapted to suit the players' ability and area available. The scoring may be designed as desired, but Fig. 1 presents a useful form.

Fig. 1 Shuffleboard markings

The game. It may be played as singles or doubles; each player or pair uses discs (quoits) of the same colour. The aim is to push the disc with the cue to land inside a plus square and at the same time to knock the opponent's disc into a negative or non-scoring position.

A wheelchair player should position himself so that he may use the cue at the side of the chair. Spastic players can build up the propelling movement with several preparatory swings. Others may need support to push the disc but this is a game which can be played even by those who cannot sit up, provided they can be propped up or even lie prone on a bed and use the cue along the side of the bed.

Billiards, darts and skittles

These are chiefly winter and wet-weather games. The majority of the handicapped can take part in billiards, though the cue may have to be adapted to enable the most severely disabled to play. Probably the greatest value of this game for the handicapped is that they may join clubs and continue playing as a leisure-time activity later, and thus be integrated into the social life of the community.

2. Non-contact games

These are games in which the opposing teams do not come into contact with one another, so that there is no possibility of players being knocked over. The teams play on either side of a net as in tenniquoits and volleyball, or each member of one team plays in turn against the whole of the opposing team as in indoor cricket and indoor rounders.

Volleyball

This game is growing in popularity in this country and it is one which lends itself to adaptation. It may be played on a regulation-size court with perhaps eight to ten players to a side, but the size of court may be adapted to suit the needs of the players and the space available. Each player should be able to cover the area of court allotted to him; those on crutches or in a wheelchair, therefore, will have a smaller area than those who move easily. Similarly, the net may be lowered but it should be sufficiently high to prevent any player being able to reach over the top of it. Instead of the standard volleyball, a light beachball may be used, or for some a balloon may be sufficient.

The game. The ball is batted with an open hand or pushed with two palms – the object is to make the ball drop in the opponent's court. Service may be with an open hand, a closed fist or, for beginners, a throw may be used. Rules for volleyball are available from the governing body of the sport, but teachers should freely adapt to suit their own pupils. For instance, normally each team may hit the ball three times before it crosses the net and no player may hit twice in succession. It may be necessary to remove restrictions on the number of hits or to extend the number. Other pupils may not have sufficient strength to bat the ball over the net; in that case, an enjoyable game can be evolved where the ball is thrown and caught.

Heading volleyball may be played by those who can stand, whether or not they have the use of the upper limbs. The game is played in much the same way as above, but a light football is usually used and the net is higher (up to 2 m).

Tenniquoits

Apparatus. One quoit (rubber or rope) and a net or rope usually 1.5 m from the ground.

Marking. The court is normally 12 m X 5.5 m for doubles and 12 m X 3 m for singles. An area 1 m away from either side of the net is marked to form a 'neutral' area.

The game. Tenniquoits may be played standing or sitting on the ground or in wheelchairs. Though normally played as a singles or doubles game, it may be played quite satisfactorily with up to four on each side. The game is played by throwing the quoit over a net or rope. The quoit must be thrown underarm. If the intention is to develop the game competitively then the established rules must be followed, but in lessons the rules should 'fit' the players, as should the size of the court and height of the net. It is a splendid game for mixed ability groups.

Table tennis

An excellent game, especially for the 'wheelchair' player who may now take part at international level if he so wishes. Competitions are arranged at area, national and international events by British Sports Association for the Disabled. The game is too well known to need description, though certain adaptations may be necessary. It is important for players in wheelchairs to have room to move their chairs easily. The table must also be very firm so that it may be grasped by wheelchair players to help them move and by those on crutches to aid their balance. Some players find using an office chair on castors particularly helpful since this allows the body to swivel with ease. Individual children soon learn how best to hold the bat to suit their stance. Wheelchair players on the whole find it easiest to hold the bat as if it were a pen whereas most players hold it as though 'shaking hands' with the bat, but it may be necessary to attach the bat in some way (for instance to the stump of a double amputee or a thalidomide victim). Similarly, children discover their own way to serve and idiosyncrasies should be accepted.

Continuous table tennis

This allows more players per table than the traditional game.

The game. The players stand round the table. One player at each end has a bat; one of these players also holds a table tennis ball. The player with the ball serves it over the net and immediately places the bat on the table and moves in a clockwise direction round the table. The next player in line picks up the bat; meanwhile the player on the other side of the table tries to return the ball. He then places his bat on the table and the next player in line takes his place. Should any player fail to return the ball, he may either lose a point or drop out of the game; the former is preferable. The winner is the player who loses the least number of points in a given time or the last player left.

Wall tennis

Another adaptation, which is a cross between table tennis and squash or fives, may be played against a wall or better still in a corner of the room, where two walls can be used. A line on the wall(s), usually about a metre from the floor, serves as a net; balls should hit the wall above it before bouncing on the floor. Players can use table tennis bats and balls, padder tennis bats and tennis balls (in which case they will play further away from the wall) or simply a ball propelled by a hand, gloved or not. Children can invent their own rules and methods of play, but the teacher may wish to allocate areas to the players and gradually lead them on to attempting rebounds from one wall to the other, as in fives or squash.

Indoor cricket (non-stop cricket)

Most children thoroughly enjoy this game. It is easily organised and may be played by the majority of the handicapped, slight adaptations being made for those in wheelchairs and those unable to run. It is a particularly useful game to play with large classes in a small area.

Apparatus. One soft ball (a tennis ball, an 'airflow' ball, even a ball made by stuffing the heel of an old sock), three stumps about $\frac{1}{3}$ of a metre in height (each mounted on a small base which may be easily knocked over) or any object about $\frac{1}{3}$ of a metre in height (such as a waste-paper bin) and a small wooden bat are required.

Markings. Simple markings are given in Fig. 2.

The game. Players are divided into a batting team and a fielding team. One player from the fielding team acts as wicket keeper and one as bowler. The rest of the fielding side scatters round the room.

The first batsman takes up a position in front of the wicket, guarding it with his bat. The rest of the batsmen stand behind their line. The ball is bowled underarm; if the batsman touches it he must run round the mark or skittle and back to the wicket, thus scoring one run. He need run only if he hits the ball. The fielders collect the ball and return it to the bowler who immediately bowls again, even if the batsman is not back. If the ball hits the wicket the batsman is out; he immedi-

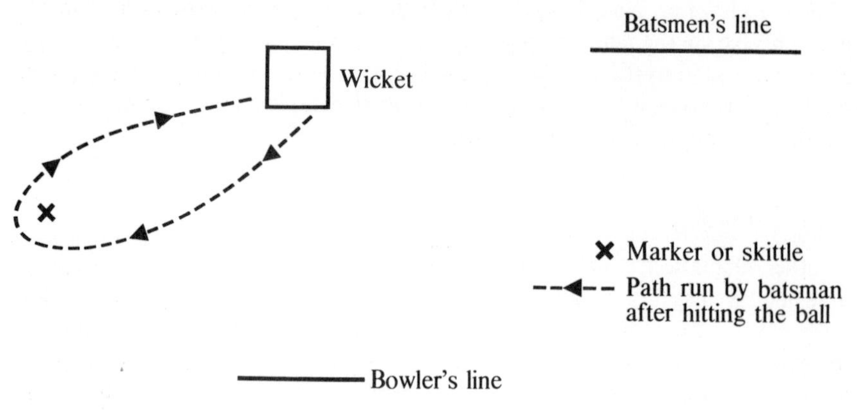

Fig. 2 Indoor cricket markings

ately drops the bat and number 2 batsman must pick it up and take up his defence. A batsman may be bowled out or caught out. The idea is to keep the batsmen 'on the hop'.

Adaptations to suit individuals may include another child (or even the teacher) acting as 'runner' for one who can bat but not run. Even children on crutches may learn to bat, bowl and even field the ball if they have had plenty of practice at basic skills.

Rounders

Rounders may be played in or out of doors but should be played outside only in warm weather since it is not a very active game. The rules of rounders are readily available, but teachers working with handicapped children should reduce the distance from base to base if necessary and increase the number of players on each team. As in non-stop cricket, substitute runners may be used.

Indoor rounders (or Danish rounders)

This is a slightly different game.

Apparatus. Rounders or padder tennis bat and an 'airflow' ball may be used. A volleyball may also be used, to be struck with the clenched fist.

Marking. Normally there are three bases (the distance apart depends on the size of the room and the skill of the players) and a batting square.

The game. There are two equal teams. The least mobile players on the fielding team should be at the bases or bowling; the more energetic can move about to field the ball. The first batsman stands in the batting square while the bowler standing near by throws the ball into the air in such a way that it will fall into the batting square if the batsman misses. After hitting the ball with stick or hand, the batsman runs round the outside of the three bases to score a rounder. Meanwhile the fielders gather the ball and pass it to the fielder at first base. He passes it to the fielder at second base, who passes it on to the third-base fielder, who returns it to the bowler. If the bowler 'touches down' before the batsman has returned to home base the batsman is out. He is also put out if he misses his swing at the ball and it falls inside the batting square. A ball which is wrongly pitched by the bowler is described as a 'no-ball'. The batting side is awarded half a rounder for three consecutive 'no-balls'. An innings is completed when all the batsmen are out and the sides change places.

Batsmen or their substitute runners should not be allowed to touch the fielders at each base as they run round, as they may knock them over. Substitute runners start from a safe place near the batting square. If the players are unskilful or lack mobility of the hips and shoulders, a volleyball may be substituted for the tennis ball and the hand used instead of a bat.

Beanbag rounders

Only a beanbag is required and no markings are necessary.

The game. The first batsman throws the beanbag as far or as well placed as he can amongst the fielders and immediately begins to run (or wheel himself) round a file made by his fellow batsmen. Every time he passes the front of the file he scores one run. Meanwhile whatever fielder picks up the beanbag remains still while the rest of the fielding team line up behind him. The team passes the beanbag from hand to hand over heads until the last one is able to hold it up and call 'stop'. The runner then goes to the end of the batting team and the next in line takes his turn to throw the beanbag. This version is particularly good for less mobile players and is a good wheelchair game.

Other versions include the ball being rolled rather than bowled and kicked rather than being batted; the runner may be allowed to stop at a post and run only when the next ball is bowled; scoring may be by shooting goals in a basket (netball ring) instead of running while the fielders, having collected the ball that the batsman has hit, stand in a circle and pass the ball round from one to another.

3. Contact games

Basketball

The major game is very vigorous and beyond the capability of all but the fittest players. There are, however, some adaptations which make it feasible for the mildly handicapped. Baskets may be lower and players may be restricted to half the court so that they play as defenders or attackers but not both.

Adapted basketball

This version is possible for players who can move easily.

Apparatus. A light plastic ball or basketball and either netball or basketball posts are required.

Marking. There are no boundaries but a centre line is drawn across the width of the pitch.

The game. Two teams normally consists of six to eight players but this may be increased. Players start in their own half of the pitch; there are two goal-keepers and the rest of the team are designated forwards or halfbacks. Players may score from anywhere on the court but it is particularly the work of forwards to score goals. The halfbacks link defence and attack; these should therefore be the most mobile players. The goal-keepers should never leave the goal they are defending, so less mobile players may be used for this position.

The game commences with a throw up or a bounce (as appropriate) between two opposing forwards who stand facing the goal they are attacking. They must touch the ball with one hand only to knock it into play. Thereafter the ball may be thrown or bounced from player to player, using one or both hands. Generally those on crutches find a one-handed pass easiest after gathering the ball to the side of the body. Teachers will need to make firm rules to prevent rough or uncontrolled play.

Wheelchair basketball

This is a very popular game which is played to international level. The international rules may be obtained from the British Sports Association for the Disabled at Stoke Mandeville. It is a splendid game for the many wheelchair players who develop strong arms through manoeuvring their chairs. Simple adaptations to normal basketball rules may easily be developed by the teacher in discussion with players. Generally these will concern how many pushes on the chair wheels are allowed without bouncing the ball and penalties for contact between chairs.

Wheelchair hockey

This, like wheelchair basketball, is an adaptation of a major game, but is usually played indoors. It is a very exciting game and so strict umpiring is necessary.

Apparatus. 'Unihoc' plastic sticks are excellent as these are lightweight, easily adapted for length and have a flat head which allows the puck to be hit by either side. If these are not available, old hockey sticks may be cut down to suit individuals. The 'puck' which replaces the hockey ball is normally a wooden block 15 cm square. A quoit could be used instead.

Marking. Goals and goal circles should be marked, together with a central line drawn across the width of the pitch.

The game. Any number may play. The teacher must judge what size teams are safe. The game begins with a 'bully' as in hockey and with all players 'on side'. Goals are scored by hits from *outside* the goal circle. Other rules should be devised to suit the ability of the players but safety requires that sticks should never be raised above the players' shoulders, that the puck be kept on the floor and that no player other than the goal-keeper should be allowed in the circle.

Ringing the stick

Apparatus. A quoit and two metre-long canes are all that is necessary. A chair is placed at either end of the gymnasium with the back of the chair against the wall.

Marking. A goal circle, usually 3 m in radius, is drawn round the chair and a central line is drawn across the width of the gymnasium.

The game. Any number from six to eleven or twelve may play on each team. If the players are in wheelchairs the number should be kept down. One player from each team stands on the chair holding a stick and facing his own team. Alternatively a wheelchair player may sit and hold the stick.

Play begins with all players standing in the half furthest from their own team player with the stick. The quoit is thrown up between one player from each side, who must stand in his own half and at the centre of the court. One of these players catches the quoit with one hand and it is then passed underarm from player to player until one is in a position to 'ring' his own stick. A goal is scored when the quoit is on the stick. Players move freely about the court, attempting to intercept the quoit, but teachers need to develop rules, in discussion with the players, appropriate to their abilities and the space available. These will include rules about stepping, or turning the wheels of a wheelchair, while holding the quoit, the length of time the quoit may be held, and passing with one hand rather than two. Strict rules are necessary to protect the stick-holder and to prevent rough play.

Basic principles applicable to all games

It has been continually emphasised that rules for all games must be adapted or developed to suit the abilities of a particular group of children. Games and teaching methods must also be designed for individuals and groups. At the same time many young people will develop sufficient skill to want to compete at local, national or international level. It is hoped that the diagram in Fig. 3 will make teachers aware of the whole spectrum of games teaching, from basic skills to opportunities for competing and umpiring.

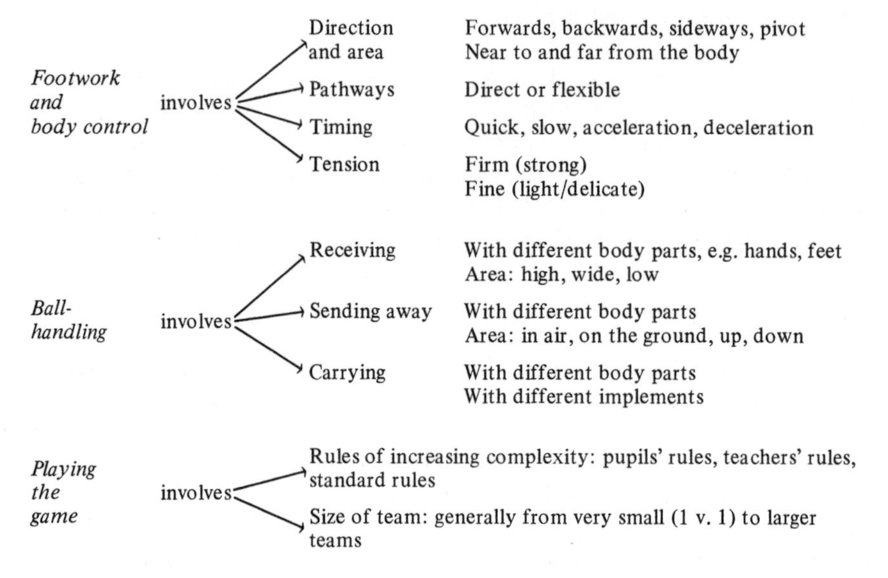

Fig. 3 Summary of principles applicable to all games (players sitting, standing or in wheelchairs)

Athletics

The value of athletics both for the disabled and for the able-bodied lies in the fact that participants can achieve personal satisfaction by competing against themselves to improve their own standard – be it distance thrown, height or distance jumped, or bettering their previous time. Through athletics physical fitness is maintained or improved and this is essential for the handicapped, especially the wheelchair patient who often has weight problems. For those who need the stimulus of competition there are excellent opportunities at school, area, national and international levels. There is some activity which almost all handicapped people can enjoy.

There are many books setting out technique and coaching of specific events; therefore it is proposed simply to list the events which have been well tried and found useful and enjoyable with handicapped pupils. The rules for competition may be obtained from the Spastic Society for the Spastic Society Games and from the British Sports Association for the Disabled for the National and International Games held at Stoke Mandeville.

Before there is any thought of competition the actions of running, jumping and throwing should be taught in junior school. Here the basic fundamentals applicable to all events are learnt.

Running

Those who are able – the blind, the deaf and the minimal brain damaged – may take part in normal running races. Each disability needs specific help; suggestions for teaching blind and deaf children appear in Chapters 6 and 7. Races are also possible for those needing support such as crutches, sticks, wheelchairs, tricycles and the various forms of boxes on wheels which enable children to be mobile. Whatever aid is used must be used correctly and the child must be in full control before being involved in competition. Any physiotherapy department will give advice on the use of various aids.

Events for blind and deaf runners include from 50 metres up to 1500 metres and even cross-country running. For those requiring aids, competition includes the 60, 80 and 100-metre dash. Even more popular are *slalom events* for wheelchair, tricycle and motorised wheelchairs. Here the athlete manoeuvres round obstacles and learns to change direction, moving forwards and backwards through narrow gates; this is excellent for developing real skill in handling the aid. In more advanced slalom courses ramps of varying heights are negotiated. A typical slalom course is given in Fig. 4. Each competitor is timed for the course. Normally one second is added for each obstacle touched or confining line broken. Obviously the winner is the competitor with the shortest time.

If a slalom course is included in an inter-school or area competition a plan of the course should be circulated well beforehand so that the athlete has time to practise the best way for him to negotiate the obstacles; in this way he learns economy of effort, so essential in his everyday life. All too often, even at area level, the organisers have to spend time teaching the circuit, and naturally some competitors are at a distinct disadvantage if others have practised and they have not.

Jumping

Jumping can be for height or length, taking off from one leg. This event is only for those capable and wishing to jump. An excellent landing area is essential but sand is not suitable unless very well looked after. Jumping is a highly co-ordinated action and neither high jump nor long jump seems very suitable for the majority of disabled people. However, if individuals do appear ready and able to jump then styles appropriate to their physique should be developed.

The basic actions for both high and long jumps may be divided into four parts:

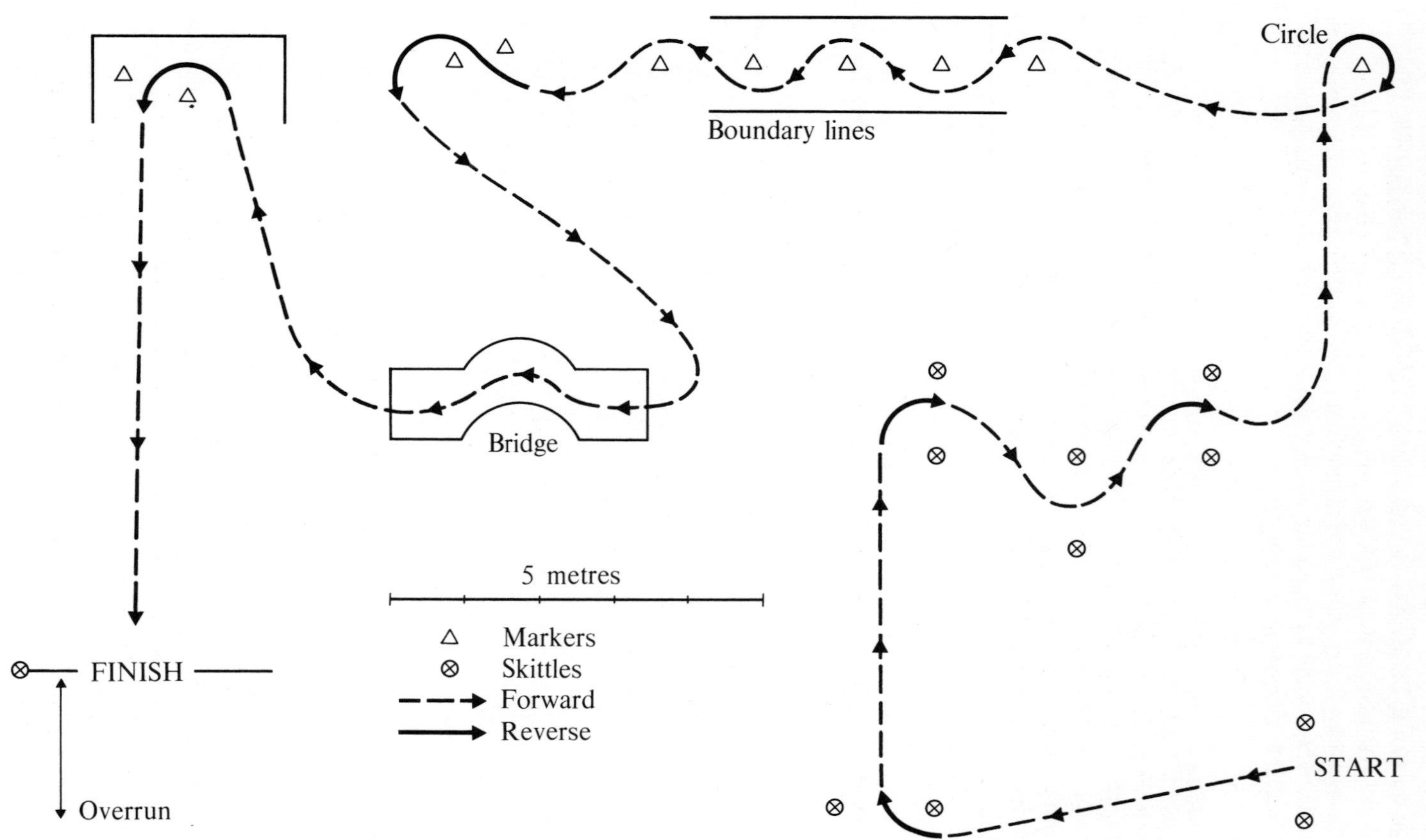

Fig. 4 A typical slalom course

1. Run-up. Speed is produced at the run-up to be converted at take-off into an upward direction for high jump and an upward and forward direction for long jump. Blind and one-legged participants may need a standing start for the high jump (a one-legged schoolboy has hopped over 1.8 m from a standing start). The one-legged athlete builds up momentum through arm swing while the blind participant can gain momentum by swinging his leading leg. Both can perform a long jump from a standing start, getting momentum from arm swing. (A one-legged first year American college student used a foot hop to approach the bar and then used a forward dive to clear it. In January 1978 he cleared over 2 m (6′ 6¾″) in this manner.)

2. Take-off. This must be from one leg.

3. Flight in the air. In the high jump the aim is to cross the bar with the body's centre of gravity as near to the bar as possible. Performers will need to find whether they can most successfully achieve this if they are 'draped' round the bar facing onto it (as in straddle), or back to it (as in the Fosbury Flop), or sideways to it (as in the Western Roll).

In the long jump the jumper may continue a running action in air (hitch kick) or he may 'hang in the air'.

4. Landing. Each style of jump has its own form of landing – in the high jump either on the take-off foot or on the opposite foot, or on the back for the Fosbury Flop or forward dive. In long jump the landing is on two feet slightly apart with the arms reaching forward. It is essential, as mentioned before, to have a safe landing area.

It should be emphasized that although many sports meetings for the disabled include long and high jumps, these are activities for the very few.

Throwing

Discus, javelin and shot are the normal throwing events but there are many variations for the less able such as light shots, medicine balls, clubs and precision javelin. Provided the implement can be held, the majority of the disabled can take part. The throwing events are very popular in competition.

The following are common to all throwing events:

1. An implement is held and thrown. The hold depends on the implement.
2. Speed is produced either by a run as in javelin, a turn in the circle, as in discus, or movement across the circle as in the shot. How speed is produced depends upon the ability of the athlete. Those in wheelchairs may twist the trunk; some prefer facing forwards, others sideways to the line of throw. Provided the wheels of the chair are not over the line and the feet do not touch the

ground, the athlete is free to experiment to find for himself the best way to throw. Some may be able to use only the swing of the arm. In the javelin throw, in order to achieve precision, the javelin is held above the head and flighted to land in the target. The blind usually take a standing throw. In the early stages of learning, canes may be used in place of a javelin and a quoit with a wooden inset instead of a discus, as this is easier to hold. For those whose hand function is impaired, ridged balls or beanbags may be used.

3. Speed is transferred to the implement and it is released. It is important that only speed that the athlete can control is produced – otherwise the implement will not be released at the right moment (this should be when the speed is maximum). The athlete must learn a great deal about timing.
4. Speed is checked to prevent the athlete's passing the throwing line or moving outside the throwing circle. From the beginning the athlete should be taught to leave from the back of the circle in both discus and shot; this is one of the rules strictly adhered to in competition and is an important safety procedure. In the heat of the moment if the athlete has made a good throw he often forgets this unless he has been well trained, and he would be disqualified for moving forward.

   The athlete is taught the checking of speed only when he has a good throwing action; otherwise the implement is released before maximum speed is achieved.

Throwing events used in disabled competitions. The throwing events used in national and international competitions for the disabled are: discus, javelin for distance and precision (aiming at a target), shot and club (which is thrown freestyle).

Additional events commonly used in competitions for children in multihandicapped schools include throwing a light ball, a cricket ball, a medicine ball and a light shot. Athletes who are severely disabled may compete in a target throw using beanbags to aim at a target drawn on the ground. This event is meant to be a substitute for the precision javelin throw; but perhaps it is better if school athletes are allowed to enter both types of competition.

Relay races

Shuttle relays appear in most sports meetings for the disabled. In these, two athletes in each team start at either end of the marked lane (60 metres is probably sufficient). A 10-metre take-over zone is marked at each end of the track. Such relays may be run for wheelchair competitors and those using other mobility aids. Competitors should be carefully matched.

Competition

Athletic competition takes place at every level, from the school sports day to the 'Olympics of the Paralysed'. But although there is increasing opportunity for competition for disabled children and adults at all levels, many authorities prefer participation sports and feel that competition can be overdone. For the few, competition provides the satisfaction that comes from success. Success is an essential ingredient, and there is nothing more demoralising than constant failure. The most important factor in providing success is the method used to grade for competition. There have been many questions about the desirability of *grading by disability*. Two third-year students at Nonington College of Physical Education decided to look at ways of *grading by ability*. Their reasons for doing this and the method they used may be helpful to other teachers; these are set out below.

Ability and disability. The students looked at nationally organised competitions and considered the method of grouping for each event. This depended upon the individual's disability; for example, children with spina bifida were grouped according to the severity of their handicap. The difference between the winners and losers in almost every event was so marked that one felt there was really no competition at all; winning was so easy for the winner, whilst winning for the loser seemed an impossible task. The students looked for an alternative approach which they hoped would allow more satisfaction for everyone. They set out to organise a 'Day of Sport' for all types of handicapped children and attempted to group them for competition according to their ability. The children's own teachers were asked to submit the best distance/time of each individual intending to compete. Before the sports day the students grouped all the children according to the information received regardless of the children's disabilities. So instead of selection according to disability they were now selected according to their ability. This produced a much closer competition and seemed to provide more individual incentive. Using this method a child works towards promotion into the next group and each goal he is aiming for does not seem so unobtainable, whereas a child who remains within his *disability* group meeting after meeting, competing with the same children time after time, may always remain a loser.

Although this method of grouping was developed particularly for inter-school competition, the lesson is relevant to all games and athletics teaching. Throughout this chapter and the whole book emphasis has been on looking at children's *ability* rather than *disability*.

Variations on athletic competition

There are a good many ways of involving handicapped children and adults in competition. Three specific suggestions only are given here.

I. Individual pentathlon

Gershman Huberman suggests an individual pentathlon for cerebral-palsied

Competition in athletic events

SINGLE EVENTS		
Throwing	**Jumping**	**Running**
Discus	*Long jump*	*On foot*
Shot	Sail	60 m
Javelin – Distance, precision	Hitch-kick	80 m
	Hang	100 m
Medicine ball		200 m
Light ball		400 m
Cricket ball		Relay
Beanbag		Distance running
Club		including
		800 m
		1500 m
	High jump	*Wheelchair and tricycle*
	Scissors	60 m
	Western roll	80 m
	Straddle	100 m
	Fosbury Flop	Relay
		Slalom
	Hop step and jump	*Electric-chair*
		Slalom

COMBINED EVENTS		
Pentathlon	**Triathlon**	**Modern pentathlon**
Speed: 100 m	Speed: 100 m	Pistol-shooting
Endurance: 1500 m	Endurance: 1500 m	Running: 200 m
Strength: shot	Strength: shot	Riding
Agility: slalom		Swimming: 25 m, 50 m
Fitness: 400 m or 50-m swim		Fencing

OFFICIALS
Clerk to the course Starter Timekeeper Judges: field events
Judges: track events

adolescents, competition being against the stop watch or tape measure. He includes activities for agility, endurance, speed, strength, physical fitness and co-ordination.

Agility	Slalom
Endurance	1500 metres
Speed	100-metre dash
Strength	Shot-put (4 kg)
Fitness and co-ordination	50-metre swim

Perhaps in the future we may see a modern pentathlon included in competition for the handicapped similar to the one in the Olympic Games. This consists of five events depicting the carrying of the King's message of ancient times: by horse, on foot, over water, and defended by pistol and sword. All these events are within the capabilities of so many disabled athletes. Interest in events of this nature is growing in schools, and this may open some splendid opportunities for competitions involving both handicapped and able-bodied young people.

II. Circuit training

This is a very popular activity in secondary schools, particularly for boys. It offers a means of competition as well as fitness training. *Circuit Training* (Morgan and Adamson, 1961) is the standard text on the subject. There are many ways of adapting the original ideas; a circuit of skill activities for a particular game or athletic events is quite useful. The child learns the skill and it is then incorporated into competition.

If the game chosen is basketball (wheelchair or adapted basketball), the skills required are ball-handling, footwork and body control or manoeuvrability of the wheelchair, and also the improvement of stamina. The skills are selected and then arranged in sequence so that a skill requiring movement is followed by one of a sedentary nature. In this way time is allowed for the less fit to recover. The activities are selected so that teams may work out the best way to perform the activity while still adhering to the rules.

Teams should consist of four members. Activities, which are numbered, are demonstrated before they are attempted. The players are given a set time for each activity and move in a clockwise direction from one activity to the next. When competition is introduced the teams have the same time for each activity and their scores are entered on a board. Activities are started by the ringing of a bell and stopped by the blast of a whistle. At the end of the circuit all scores are added and a winning team emerges.

A specimen circuit

Fig. 5 sets out a sample circuit of eight activities designed to improve basketball skills and the players' stamina. Although the verbs 'stand' and 'run' are used in the descriptions below, all activities are equally suitable for competitors in wheelchairs.

1. Stationary shot. Numbered circles are arranged around the shooting area. Each player with a ball stands in one of the circles numbered 1. After a successful or unsuccessful shot at the goal the shooter collects his own ball. After a successful shot he moves on to a circle numbered 2, then 3, and so on. Scores of individuals are added together and entered on the score board.

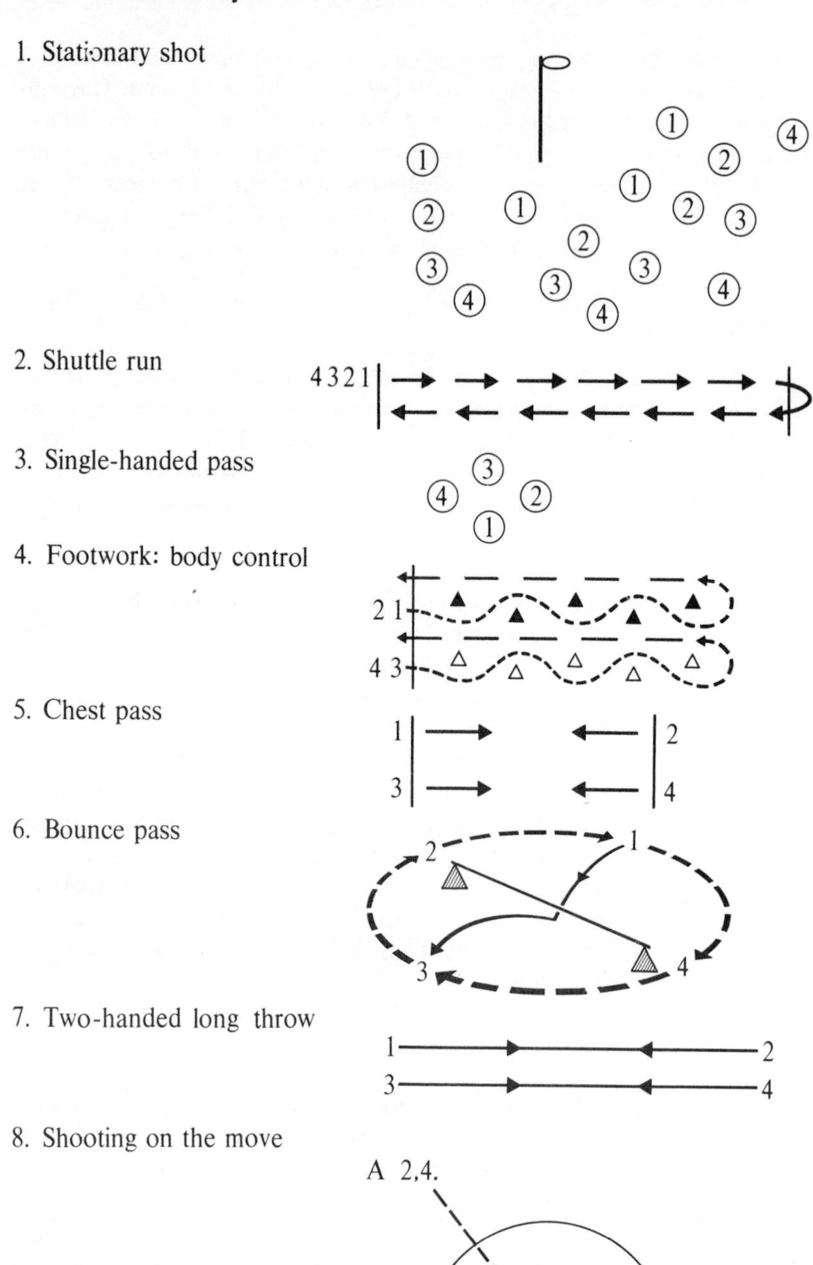

Fig. 5 Circuit for basketball skills (players on feet or in wheelchairs)

2. *Shuttle run.* A line is drawn at either end of the gymnasium, well away from the wall. The players run from one line to the other and back again, scoring a point for each run completed within the given time. If players are in wheelchairs this could be organised as a shuttle relay (see diagram).

3. *Single-handed pass.* Four circles are drawn on the ground some distance from each other and a player stands in each circle. One player has a ball which is passed round the circle. One point is scored when the round is completed. One version involves using the right hand to pass for the first round and the left hand for the second but this may be adapted to suit the players' ability.

4. *Footwork: body control.* A starting line is drawn and two lines of skittles are set out as in the diagram. Players 1 and 2 stand facing one line of skittles, and 3 and 4 face the other line. As soon as 1 and 3 have started to run in and out of the line of skittles facing them, 2 and 4 may begin to run. At the far end of the line the players run down the side of the skittles, back to the starting line. One point is scored for each completed run and the scores are added together.

5. *Chest-pass.* Players face each other in pairs and chest-pass a basketball between them. One point is scored each time the ball is caught and the scores of the two team-mates added together.

6. *Bounce-pass.* Two skittles are placed with a long cane balanced on top. Players are arranged round the apparatus, as in the diagram. Player 1 bounces the ball under the cane to player 3 and moves to take the place of player 4; player 2 moves forward to collect the ball, which 3 has bounced back under the cane, and bounces it back to player 4, who has moved forward (i.e. players move clockwise). Each time the ball is bounced and caught one point is scored. If the cane is knocked off that score does not count.

7. *Two-handed long throw.* Players stand in pairs facing each other across the width of the gymnasium and pass a basketball back and forth from behind the head, using two hands. One point is scored for each catch and the scores of the pairs are added together.

8. *Shooting on the move.* The diagram shows one way of organising a drill which involves a player moving to receive a ball and taking a quick shot at a goal. Two players stand outside the goal circle at A and two outside the circle at B. Player 1 at B throws the ball into the circle while player 2 runs from A into the circle to catch the ball and shoot at goal. Player 2 then runs to collect the ball from the goal and passes it to player 3. Players 3 and 4 repeat the drill, while player 1 moves to A and player 2 moves to B, so that each player has a turn at catching and shooting at goal. One point is scored for each successful goal.

III. 'It's a knockout'

Readers will be familiar with this 'fun' type of competition on television. Teachers and their pupils will have their own ideas for items to include in their version of the game. A specimen programme planned by two Nonington College students, and successfully used with a large group of children from handicapped schools in Kent, may help inspire readers to develop their own school or inter-school competition; details are set out below. In this particular event every member of a team took part in at least two events and a team game of handball in the college pool brought the day to a climax.

In the sports hall/on a field

1. Frog in the field. One competitor is blindfolded and wears swimming flippers on hands and feet. All round him are balloons. His partner shouts instructions through a megaphone to lead him to the balloons. One point is scored for each balloon the blindfolded player bursts.

2. Wimbledon capers. Four members of a team take part in this activity. One player has a basket full of tennis balls which he feeds one at a time to another player who, using a tennis racquet, hits the ball; the ball then has to be caught in a basket by one of the two other members of the team. One point is scored for each ball caught.

3. The hungry people. Each team fields four competitors. Each pair is linked in some way (rings and string joining nearest wrists has been tried successfully). The first pair goes through an obstacle course and returns to the start before the next pair may begin. Every section of the obstacle course must be completed successfully by both couples for the 'run' to count. The course consists of buns on a string (the couple jump from a bench to bite the dangling bun – a crash mat for landing from the jump is necessary), apples in a bowl of water (to be picked out with the teeth), a balloon (to be blown up and burst) and a saucerful of flour with squares of chocolate in it (each player to find a square with his teeth). This game causes much hilarity and excitement but of course any form of 'obstacle course' may be used. The winning team is the one to successfully complete the course in the shortest time.

4. Crazy cricket. This game is similar to beanbag rounders described earlier in the chapter (p. 65), but instead of a beanbag being thrown a 'giant golf ball' is hit with a giant golf club. The winning team is the one to score the highest number of 'runs' in the time allowed. This game is particularly suitable for wheelchair competitors.

In the swimming pool

1. The raft race (for competent swimmers only). Each team has four competitors. One swimmer is at the deep end of the pool on an inflatable bed (li-lo). The others are spaced at intervals down the pool, treading water (though the fourth player could be standing in the shallow end). The swimmer on the inflatable bed uses his hands to scull up the pool and 'rescues' each of his team mates in turn. When all are on the 'raft' they paddle it back to the start. The winning team is the one to complete the course in the shortest time with all aboard.

2. Mini-marathon. (Since this is played in the shallow end of the pool it is suitable for beginner swimmers.) Each team provides four competitors. Four from one team have floats tied on top of their heads on which they have to balance paper cups while they walk across the width of the pool. Meanwhile four members of another team stand on the side with detergent bottles filled with water which they squirt at the cups, trying to knock them over. Having safely landed (or lost) a paper cup on the other side of the pool, the competitor returns for another. The winning team is the one with the greatest number of cups safely delivered in the time available.

3. Water handball. This is played in the shallow end of the pool and players walk or swim. The ball is passed from hand to hand; goals are scored by shooting at a netball post standing at the side of the pool. A skittle or some other object could be used for a goal if desired. No one is allowed to travel while holding the ball or to touch another player.

This then describes one 'It's a knockout' afternoon in which secondary-school-age children with a variety of abilities and disabilities took part. Preparation for the games involved training in skills; the games themselves brought pupils from a number of schools together to compete, to have fun and, above all, to mix with one another.

Conclusion

Games and athletics involve the basic principles of movement. A child should be guided to discover the best way he can respond to a set task. It cannot be stressed too strongly that he should be *taught* skills and techniques rather than simply be allowed to play a game. Through participation in games and athletics a child learns economy of effort, which is so essential in everyday life. The programme should be adapted to suit the ability and the needs of the individual and, though basic skills need to be taught, the actual activities need to be varied from day to day or both teacher and child will become bored. The teacher must build up a child's confidence so that he will approach life with enthusiasm and without fear. Most children find it difficult to resist the challenge of games, and participation brings physical, psychological and social benefits. Weak muscles are strengthened, joint mobility is improved and general fitness is developed; success brings confidence and disabilities may be forgotten in fun and excitement; games play and competition, whether at the 'Olympics of the Paralysed' or in the school 'It's a knockout', help to develop confidence in inter-personal relationships.

Sadly, too many people still believe that the way to help physically handicapped children is to do things for them and to protect them. It is perhaps worth bearing in mind the old Chinese proverb: 'Give a man a fish and you feed him for one day: teach a man to fish and you feed him for life.' Let us give the children in our care the chance to become as self-sufficient as possible. Games and athletics may well play a valuable part.

5 Accent on adventure: an account of outdoor pursuits

PATRICK BELSHAW

There are many possible openings to this chapter. I could begin by examining the philosophical basis of my programme content. On the other hand the Plowden report reminds us that 'at the heart of the educational process lies the child'; I could – perhaps, indeed, I properly should – begin with the child and his needs. Or I could begin with adventure itself and question whether it constitutes one of those needs – an exercise that would demand some examination of the concept of 'need' and 'adventure'. Then again, I ought perhaps to remember that I am dealing with the handicapped child and that these are ordinary children with extraordinary needs. Thus I could begin by looking at the needs of the physically handicapped child, to determine which are 'extraordinary' and which, if any, are common to all children. Finally, accepting the existence of certain needs, I could begin by considering the role of outdoor pursuits as a vehicle for meeting those needs. This would necessarily involve a definition of what we mean by the term 'outdoor pursuits'. Having thus presented the major areas to be covered, I begin with the semantic problem.

What is meant by 'outdoor pursuits'?

Of course we all know what we mean by 'outdoor pursuits' – yet even bodies as august as the British Association of Advisors and Lecturers of Physical Education and the Physical Education Association can apparently be unmindful of possible differences in the interpretation of this term. In their joint report published in 1969 satisfaction was expressed in 'the growing use of outdoor pursuits for handicapped children', and 'some evidence' was offered 'that the younger children also participate' (*National Survey of PE for Handicapped Children*). However, this evidence is questionable because there can be a great difference between the nursery–infant teacher's interpretation of terms like 'climbing', 'walking', 'outdoor pursuits' and 'outdoor activities' and that of, say, a PE specialist in a secondary school.

The report uses the terms 'outdoor pursuits' and 'outdoor activities' synonymously; perhaps they are synonymous in the minds of physical educationists. But as Parker and Meldrum point out in their book, *Outdoor Education*, other terms often used loosely as synonyms (e.g. 'outdoor sports' and 'outward bound') can only cause confusion. Parker and Meldrum go on to define outdoor pursuits as 'necessarily physically demanding undertakings performed outside the classroom', relying 'more on the natural environment than on artificial situations, and for which overt competition is not an essential feature'. Realising that this represents a very wide range of activities (including, presumably, fishing, jogging, cycling, horse riding, sledging, rambling, swimming etc.), they then suggest that the field can be 'narrowed a little by admitting the element of danger which is implied in "adventure training" '. This, I assume, leaves us with what they later refer to as 'outdoor adventure pursuits': namely, skiing, sailing, climbing, canoeing and caving (in descending order of popularity, according to their figures).

Parker and Meldrum appear to rest their case at this point, which is rather disappointing because so many questions are left undebated. For example, do outdoor pursuits have to be 'necessarily physically demanding' – thus excluding fishing, for example? And – to anticipate the protest that fishing is not always contemplative – isn't the term 'physically demanding' relative, anyway? (To a child with a cardiac handicap, certain phases of fishing could well impose physical demands close to the limit of his tolerance.)

Also, what of this 'element of danger'? By definition, does danger not involve risk – and when you are responsible for the well being of others is not risk a luxury you can ill afford? As far as the physically handicapped are concerned, the view of the DES on this matter is unequivocal:

> No physically handicapped child should be subjected to any unnecessary risk to life or limb in an enthusiastic endeavour to provide a 'normal' life for him. A sensible balance must be struck between the foreseeable risks of any particular physical exercise and the gain the child may be expected to derive from it.
> (*DES, Physical Education for the Physically Handicapped*)

The Department of Education and Science has produced a pamphlet on safety (1972), and associations like the National Association for Outdoor Education and a number of LEA's have also published advice and regulations. Cumbria's pamphlet 'Safety Out-of-Doors' includes the phrase 'danger under control' as a definition of adventure, and stresses that all-important balance required 'to reduce the risk to acceptable limits whilst still retaining the adventure'.

More on the subject of adventure later; but if certain activities are to be labelled 'adventurous' and others not, then I think we have to be clear that the criteria being used are surely highly personal. For example, just to spend a night under canvas can mean real adventure to a child who has never been away from home before, whereas, at the other end of the spectrum, it may be possible to become almost blasé about a bivouac on an exposed face at 3,000 m above sea level! Sir Edmund Hillary in *Nothing Venture Nothing Win* (Hodder and Stoughton, 1975) reminds us that 'even the mediocre can have adventure, and even the fearful can achieve'. Anderson, in *The Ulysses Factor*, emphasises the personal, relative dimension of an adventure when he says: 'Physical discovery is personal. It does not lessen a child's sense of discovery in crawling across a room that the other occupants of the house know every stick of furniture', and 'the challenge is in oneself'.

Clearly, more discussion on the nature of outdoor pursuits is necessary. In dealing with the handicapped in general, and with the physically handicapped in particular, we should accept a wider notion of outdoor pursuits than the 'popular group' concept presented in most texts. In the following classification, category I activities will be seen to be largely outside the scope of our work with the handicapped; but category III activities, in particular, constitute a very fruitful field.

I. Minority specialist pursuits

Water-skiing
Scuba (i.e. using 'self-contained underwater breathing apparatus')
Gliding
Hang-gliding
Surfing etc.

II. Popular specialist pursuits

Skiing, including dry and grass
Sailing
Mountain activities: (*a*) Rock-climbing
(*b*) General mountaineering, including winter mountaineering
(*c*) Mountain- and fell-walking
Canoeing
Caving
Pony-trekking
Orienteering
Camping (expedition)

III. Largely recreational pursuits

(including some specialist elements)
Boating
Swimming (outdoor; recreational)
Cycling
Camping (recreational)
Skating (outdoors) on rollers and, in season, on ice
Walking
Angling and fishing generally
Archery (recreational), including target and field

Snow activities (in season): Sledging
Sliding
Tray-riding
Poly-bagging

Rambling
Snorkelling etc.

The requirements for inclusion in these lists are that all activities must be conducted out-of-doors and in the natural environment as far as possible. Team games are excluded, and personal challenge and recreation replace overt competition. The accent is on enjoyable participation and personal satisfaction rather than on the elitist achievement of set standards.

This is the (somewhat personal) concept of outdoor pursuits that will serve as a reference point in this account, and on which I would wish to base my work with the handicapped. If one accepts the more traditional view of outdoor pursuits and centres one's work on the major activities only, one surely denies a large proportion of physically handicapped children the opportunity of involvement in what I consider to be an important theatre of educational experience. Having made this claim, I must obviously justify it by examining the degree to which the aims of outdoor pursuits appear to satisfy the special needs of the physically handicapped.

The aims of outdoor pursuits

These may be listed as follows:

1. To afford enjoyment and satisfaction;
2. To offer opportunities for the acquisition of new skills;
3. To offer opportunities for the improvement of interpersonal relationships and the process of socialization;
4. To help improve aesthetic awareness;
5. To promote a deeper knowledge and regard for the countryside;
6. To help improve awareness of the importance of conservation;
7. To offer scope for the development of self-reliance and the exercising of initiative;
8. To offer opportunities for the development of greater self-awareness;
9. To contribute to an improvement in general health, and to help bring individuals closer to 'total fitness' as a concept and in reality;
10. To afford opportunities for adventure, excitement and challenge.

Presumably, we would all accept that the handicapped child has a right . . .

to a life on which his handicap casts no shadow, but which is full day by day with those things which make it worth while . . . a life in which these things bring continually increasing growth, richness, release of energies, joy in achievement. (White House Conference Report 1930: 'White House Conference on Child Health and Protection')

This 'joy in achievement', this satisfaction to be derived from exertion and the mastery of techniques, is a need common to us all; and outdoor pursuits certainly offer the requisite wide range of activities and experiences – many of them intrinsically enjoyable – to cater for this need.

These activities and experiences involve opportunities for attempting and mastering a new range of skills and techniques, thus increasing the likelihood that every handicapped child will find *something* he can do. I subscribe to the view expressed throughout this book that emphasis should be on ability rather than disability and that we should look for activities a child can do rather than think of those he cannot. The field of outdoor pursuits offers plenty of opportunities for children to make use of their remaining abilities and to compensate for loss or diminution of one part of the body by their involvement in an activity that makes demands on a different part.

The third aim on the list is related to the eighth, in that an accurate awareness (and acceptance) of self is crucial in one's relationships with others. Some people still maintain that outdoor pursuits develop character. Well, who knows, since there is no evidence either way? But it may be more accurate to say that outdoor pursuits *reveal* character – perhaps to a degree unequalled in any other educational activity. Certainly, where the challenges are largely 'in oneself', an improvement in self-knowledge seems a logical possibility – and, as indicated in Chapter 1, there is some evidence that greater clarity of the body image may help to alleviate some of the learning difficulties of the handicapped child, too.

It has been said that for many people their handicap is 'more social than physical'; few are able to demonstrate the high level of adjustment shown by one multiple sclerotic sufferer who wrote:

Both healthy minds and healthy bodies may be crippled. The fact that 'normal' people can get around, can see, can hear, doesn't mean that they are seeing or hearing. They can be very blind to the things that spoil their happiness, very deaf to the pleas of others for kindness; when I think of them I do not feel any more crippled or disabled than they. Perhaps in some small way I can be the means of opening their eyes to the beauties around us; things like a warm handclasp, a voice that is anxious to cheer, a spring breeze, music to listen to, a friendly nod. These people are important to me and I feel that I can help them.
(Henrich and Knegel, eds., *Experiments in Survival*)

I quote this passage at length because it seems to me that here is a message for us all. Certainly, the words represent a statement of what is largely my philosophy. The last sentence is particularly important. It underlines the need for the handicapped to take positive steps themselves towards adjustment and integration. It stresses the taking of initiative – which relates to the seventh aim on my list – and it implies a sense of responsibility. Outdoor pursuits offer significant opportunities for handicapped children to gain self-reliance and exercise initiative, and to come to a better understanding of themselves and others.

With regard to aims four, five and six, by involving the handicapped in a variety of activities – in different countryside environments, if possible – we are satisfying many of the needs that Jackson (in *Special Education in England and Wales*) identifies so clearly;

> One of the aims of any school for the physically handicapped is to try to give the children the experiences which their physical handicap has caused them to miss. In the residential school for the physically handicapped this need becomes particularly urgent and special efforts need to be made both to provide adequate play-experience and to keep the child in touch with the workaday world by outside visits, attempts at shopping – and meeting new people.

In connection with the contribution to health and fitness as an aim (number nine), I deliberately use the term 'total fitness', which is now widely used to describe a state of physical and mental harmony. Most physical educationalists have 'total fitness' as an aim but this concept is especially important when dealing with physically handicapped children. If for example one takes a complaint like bronchial asthma, an attack may be brought on not only by some type of physical stimulus but also by mental fatigue or emotional stress.

The importance of considering the effects of a physical education programme on the whole child is stressed again and again throughout this book; outdoor pursuits seem to offer an eminently suitable vehicle through which total fitness may be approached. Physical exertion in clean air and (one hopes!) sunshine; the mental stimulation to be gained from facing challenge; the enjoyment; the social emphasis – all these will help bring the handicapped closer to that state of total fitness to which, presumably, we all aspire.

My tenth and last aim concerns adventure, which is popularly thought to be such a major element of outdoor pursuits. Its definition includes such emotive words and phrases as 'risk', 'danger', 'daring enterprise' and 'hazardous activity' – all of them almost calculated to make one reach for one's copy of *Teachers and the Law*! For some, further alarm may be spread by Mortlock's definition (quoted in Parker and Meldrum) of adventure: 'involvement in a situation that calls for all, or nearly all, a person's physical and mental resources to be utilized in surviving the situation'. How can one gauge the limit of a person's physical and mental resources? Mortlock may possibly cause further consternation by his suggestion that fear is a necessary ingredient of adventure.

Yet one may be reassured by psychologists such as Woodworth and Marquis, who point out that

> Strange as it may seem, many favourite forms of play and recreation depend on

fear. The chutes, roller coasters, etc. of the amusement parks would have no attraction if they had no thrill; and the thrill is a form of fear. You experience some of the thrill of danger while knowing that the danger is not very real. Probably the sense of danger would not be worth much by itself, but danger quickly followed by the joy of escape is highly satisfactory. The same can be said of any adventurous sport. (*Psychology*, 1972)

Even so, perhaps Mortlock occupies a position towards one end of a spectrum, while those who simply equate 'novelty' with adventure occupy a position at the other. I believe, with Anderson, that discovery is personal. In the same way, I believe that concepts like 'challenge' and 'adventure' are also personal. In my view, there exists a *spectrum of adventure*; according to your strength, stamina, training, expertise, previous experience (and perhaps 'spirit' and 'courage') – and certainly your degree of handicap – there is a position on the spectrum that, for you, represents real adventure. If your name is John Ridgway or Chay Blyth you will occupy a position at the perilous expedition end: if you are a ten-year-old suffering from spina bifida, two hands on an oar during a crossing of the small school 'lake' could constitute just as much of an adventure. Further, your position on the spectrum is not constant. For not only can you move along a notch or two as you acquire more experience, but your position may also change according to the nature of the activity involved. Thus, a man may be in an 'Eiger direct' position as far as mountaineering is concerned; but the same man, conceivably, could find even a modest sea-canoeing expedition quite a challenge – especially if he happened to be an indifferent swimmer and prone to seasickness!

Like everyone else a physically handicapped person needs to explore and to discover himself, but more than most people he needs to be presented with opportunities that will provide a stimulus. Anderson writes that 'although "the Ulysses factor" (i.e. the exploring instinct) may be dormant in a great many individuals, it will unconsciously respond to some exploit that excites it' – thus emphasising the importance of capturing imaginations. This is particularly pertinent in the case of the physically handicapped, because occasionally one finds oneself struggling against years of conditioned behaviour, and minds as well as bodies need unfettering. This may take time.

If a teacher takes a broad view of outdoor pursuits, as suggested above, he can make available such a wide range of experiences and pursuits that every child can find an adventure which for him is a real challenge however modest it may seem to others.

This then is my view of the value of outdoor pursuits for the physically handicapped. I regard involvement in such pursuits neither as a panacea nor as an alternative to other physical activities. It simply affords further opportunities for personal and social enrichment: another dimension. Let me now turn to a consideration of some of the important influences operating on the provision of this extra dimension of experience.

Some factors influencing an adventure programme

In a society which offers such safety and security the questing spirit of adventure must be provided for.

(Extract from a camp school information sheet, Lancashire LEA)

The dilemma facing a school is that on the one hand it must be able to positively guarantee conditions of safety and security and on the other hand, if it is a good school, it will be eager to ensure that this 'questing spirit' is catered for. The degree to which these two may be seen to be compatible will depend on one's interpretation of 'safety' and 'adventure', and on judgement in balancing risk and possible benefits. The rather awesome responsibility for these interpretations and judgements rests (in a school for the physically handicapped ['PH school']) with medical officers and with teachers and their advisers. Not surprisingly, decisions are not to be made lightly. Even a minimal risk will be taken only on the basis of a strong commitment to a set of beliefs, so that a clear philosophy of one's work is called for. Philosophies do not grow overnight; they are shaped by experience and certainly by the situation in which they are going to operate. But whilst a philosophy is developing the practical use of resources and environment to meet the needs of the children has to be faced. One must begin the development of an adventure programme modestly and cautiously. From the onset the school and its environment will be a major factor.

Residential schools, for example, may present their own special problems in other directions, but as far as the outdoor pursuits programme is concerned they generally offer considerable advantages over the day school. Most pursuits are time-consuming and cannot be readily accommodated within normal timetable blocks: thus there tends to be a heavy emphasis on evening and weekend participation. The residential school can obviously permit this so much more easily. Lines between curricular- and extra-curricular activities can become encouragingly blurred, especially with such a strong and obvious recreative element involved; and with time not a problem, both content and organization of an adventure programme should benefit.

A second point concerns the location of a school. Any programme of outdoor pursuits ideally should be related to activities that can take place in three main environments:

1. The school environment: what the school and its environs has to offer;
2. The local environment: within, say, a 16-km radius, thus permitting cheap and easy access;
3. The wider environment: so far away that only occasional visits can be afforded; usually used for annual camps, field weeks etc.

Obviously, the more facilities there are on one's doorstep the more money and time can be saved. Therefore, as far as their value to the teacher and the children is concerned, these three spheres should be considered in the order listed above, i.e. with the school and local environments the main interest.

Because of transport considerations, day schools have to be close to the centres of population; therefore many important natural features (lake, river, stream, sea, hill, dale, moorland, woodland, open ground, farmland, outcrop etc.) could well lie outside their local environment. Residential schools, on the other hand, are often situated either in rural settings, or on the fringe, with easy access to the countryside and to many of the natural facilities one needs.

Again, residential schools are so often better endowed with spacious grounds. For example, I was fortunate enough to commence my work with the physically handicapped in a school whose outdoor facilities consisted of some twenty acres of ground, including lawns, woodland, rough pasture, a pond, a large garden, a stream, a small lake, tarmacadamed drives and courtyards – even stables! To have at my disposal such a rich and varied environment without having to set foot outside the premises had a profound effect upon the philosophy underlying the whole of my programme of physical education, and on its outdoor pursuits component in particular. But more of this later.

Indoor facilities can also be of importance – if only, in this context, because a lack of them may cause a teacher to focus his work out-of-doors wherever possible! Here, the day school may score over the residential school, because the likelihood of its being functionally built is perhaps greater. Good indoor facilities are not only desirable to support a sound general programme of physical education; they also have a useful back-up role to play in outdoor pursuits. Obvious examples are the indoor heated pool, providing water confidence, aquatic skills and capsize practice; and the hall/gymnasium, where further confidence and skill of a different type may be acquired, and where conditioning and testing (e.g. for the Duke of Edinburgh Award Scheme) may be carried out.

The importance of links between school and outside bodies must be noted. They are valuable for a number of reasons:

1. They enable the school to obtain useful campsite, mooring, stabling facilities etc.
2. Whilst a school may aim to acquire all its own gear, this is a gradual process – and meanwhile these links facilitate the borrowing of items like boats, tents etc.
3. They can provide access permission, often so vital for water activities.
4. They can provide a source of assistance and expertise, e.g. the local Rotary Club providing transport to camp; the local branch of the Red Cross Society offering a first-aid course (such as in the Duke of Edinburgh Award Scheme, 'Service' section); a member of the local Women's Institute assisting with the 'Design for Living' section of the Duke of Edinburgh's Scheme; responsible volunteers helping to create a one-to-one ratio for a 'risks' activity.
5. Links with other schools and youth organisations afford vital opportunities

for the physically handicapped to work and play with so-called 'normals'. This helps both sections of the community to integrate more successfully. (In this context the growth of Physically Handicapped and Able-Bodied groups described in Chapter 9 is to be welcomed.)

6. Such links can provide the necessary opportunities for the physically handicapped themselves to be of service to the community, perhaps developing as a consequence of involvement in the Duke of Edinburgh Scheme, 'Service' section.
7. Outside bodies may occasionally help to raise funds that can be used to purchase much-needed equipment. (LEAs are currently finding it impossible to provide what some unfortunately regard as 'extras', so the PTA and other fund-raising agencies could be important to a programme.)

The influence of the staff on a school's programme is of obvious importance. I use the word 'staff' deliberately to embrace all employees at the school who will come into contact with the children. Policy-making may lie only with medical and teaching personnel; but if the programme devised by these professionals is to be really effective it requires the understanding and co-operation of every adult member of the community. Any accent placed on adventure, challenge, determination, self-reliance and exploration should be reflected by everyone's work. A programme may look fine on paper – but it won't work to full advantage if, for example, the school matron is over-protective; or if your medical ancillaries will cosset and carry instead of offering little challenges which will encourage children to move for themselves; or if your groundsman objects to the building of dens in the wood. Commitment and enthusiasm will soon permeate from the top, of course; but simple explanations of the basic philosophy may prove a useful supplement.

One's philosophy may, as I have indicated, be influenced by various environmental factors. Precisely *how* these influences work, of course, is a very individual affair, depending on background, training, personal experience and personality. I can describe only to some extent how my own thinking was shaped.

As a physical educationist I had to be concerned with the physical education programme as a whole, and not simply with the outdoor pursuits component. Having established fairly quickly what the children *could not do*, I turned to the problem of identifying exactly what they *could do*. Here I found the observation of children at play very useful. Movement certainly featured in this play – but, for some, not always to a degree that matched their functional ability: they needed more encouragement to move. So, indoors and outside, natural movement of any kind was actively encouraged as often as possible.

I began, then, with the conviction that, initially, any movement is desirable for those who may previously have been largely inactive. Developing from this, if the drive of play could be harnessed to create more structured forms of movement we might then begin to tackle disability problems on a more economical and scientific basis, and at the same time retain children's interest. In other words the premise became: 'all *movement* is good – but some *movements* are better than others'.

Numerous examples of the relationship between natural movement and structured movements are offered below:

Natural movement and play forms		**Structured movements (that could be incorporated into a programme)**
Bouncing on beds	developing into	Trampolining
Building dens	" "	Camping
Climbing stairs	" "	Climbing skills on climbing apparatus
Making and using bows and arrows	" "	Archery
Wheelchair skills	" "	Games (netball, hockey etc.) races & obstacle courses
Climbing trees	" "	Rock-climbing
Making and throwing spears and other missiles	" "	Athletic throwing events: javelin, shot & discus
Pond-dipping & net-fishing	" "	Angling
'Messing about in boats'	" "	Canoeing & sailing
Walking	" "	Rambling & hiking
Bath and water play	" "	Swimming & snorkelling
Sliding	" "	Skiing
Messing about on wheels	" "	Bicycling, tricycling, roller skating, trolleying etc.
Romping	" "	Wrestling
Exploring school grounds via local walks, bike and chair rides	" "	Walking, cycling, trekking and canoeing expeditions

Awareness of this relationship between natural and structured movements helped me to form a concept of outdoor pursuits for the physically handicapped in which play could take its place alongside organised activity – and in which 'adventure' and 'challenge' were not simply seen as prerogatives of the small minority who could attempt canoe expeditions, rock-climbing, and the like, but were seen to be possible *on a personal level* for every child in the school.

The emphasis I gave to outdoor work, while stemming from my own interest in the outdoors, probably got its most significant boost from my involvement in the Duke of Edinburgh Award Scheme. Here was a chance to prove – within a nationally known structure already established for the able-bodied – that a programme could be adapted to provide equal challenge to individuals whatever the nature of their handicap. In the early 1960s I suppose one was helping to pioneer this type of work. Later, the Award Scheme Office was able to offer guidance:

> any diminution of the physical challenge and effort necessitated by the young person's handicap should be compensated for by an additional demand in another aspect of the activity.

In the physically demanding sections of the Scheme we experimented with modifications to suit the needs of individuals, but we conformed to the principle that 'effort and persistence involved must equate with that of an able-bodied participant doing this section . . . as far as this is measurable'. When I say 'we' I refer to the fact that often it was the children themselves who set their own harsh standards.

Involvement in the scheme taught me a great deal, but I later reluctantly abandoned it in order to broaden the scope for outdoor activities with a much wider section of the school population.

By this time, the excursion from school – to camp, to canoe, to walk, to mix with the able-bodied – had become an important feature of the programme I was involved in. There were perhaps two main reasons for this:

1. It afforded opportunities for greater understanding and smoother integration – for the so-called 'normal' children, as well as for the handicapped.
2. It provided an important antidote to any tendency to insularity. When the school environment is rich, there is a temptation to be self-contained – to close your eyes and your doors to the world outside and become totally absorbed in the micro-society within. The school grounds and immediate environs probably offered enough challenge and adventure for every child in the community. After all, they had a pool to swim in; a lake to canoe on; trees to climb and swing from; fields to camp in; lawns to practise archery on; a trout-stocked stream to fish in; banks to slide down; undergrowth to make dens in; and smooth paths to run wheels on: all this before they need even set foot or wheel outside the gate – and outside lay the beautiful countryside of North Yorkshire! Idyllic, perhaps? A veritable paradise. Yet without contact with the outside world into which these children would soon be plunged it would have been cloud-cuckoo-land.

I have briefly described some aspects of a developing philosophy and possible influences on it. The programme grows along with, and out of, that philosophy. It now remains to look at the content of this programme.

Possible content of an adventure programme

Programme content is drawn from any activity that carries a potential to challenge and excite an individual, at whatever personal level may be involved – however 'tame' that experience may appear to others. Because of the wide range of handicap and the subtle degrees of disability found in any school for the physically handicapped, the content spectrum is correspondingly broad. For economy as much as for interest, I have grouped together activities that are related in some way.

Adventure through aquatics

Water holds a fascination for all children, and water activities of different types represent a major part of any programme. These activities are really founded on work done in the swimming pool, through which almost all physically handicapped children may acquire what I call 'water wisdom'. The acquisition of awareness and confidence as well as a range of skills in water are described in Chapter 8.

When weather conditions permit, outdoor swimming may be attempted. Apart from the extra exhilaration of swimming in the open air, confidence in colder water is really a prerequisite for those intending to canoe or sail. Snorkelling, too, should be considered: it opens up an exciting new world underwater, and, as Croucher points out in *Outdoor Pursuits for Disabled People*, the fact that one swims on the surface without lifting the head to breathe can be an advantage for people with certain handicaps.

The importance of just 'messing about in boats' cannot be overrated because it offers such a range of adventure experiences, even for the severely handicapped. In a safe environment, with adequate adult supervision and assistance, anything that floats with 100% certainty may be used (rowing boats, rubber dinghies, rafts etc.), offering degrees of physical involvement dependent on the disabilities of the children. Sometimes bodies may have to play a passive role: but what adventures can be acted out in the mind!

Sailing and canoeing provide more technical extensions to this experience. Whilst helming does demand only light functional restriction, children with more restricting handicaps can form the crew; and closed-cell foam and other padding may be used to provide greater comfort and safety in the sailing dinghy. Upper-limb mobility is all that is needed for paddling a canoe, and for children who lack the required degree of co-ordination simple outriggers may be attached to the boat. Canoeing lends itself superbly to the simple (or more advanced) river expedition, in which the experience of camping – and indeed, field studies – may also be combined. In both sailing and canoeing (using 'doubles') the grouping of fully-ambulant with non-ambulant children may solve a number of problems.

Adventure through hunting, shooting and fishing

Man's hunt for his quarry began on foot, and in orienteering we find an element of the thrill of the 'chase'. The recently developed 'wayfaring' courses may be highly appropriate for those children with sufficient intelligence to read a map and use a compass. The sport can begin with tracking games, like 'hare and hounds', in which children in wheelchairs can participate, leading to simple compass games in the school grounds or the local park. In these activities, ambulant 'pushers' can team up with children in wheelchairs. (Caution: wheelchairs can have interesting effects on compass needles!) Orienteering courses for asthmatics can be devised in which the emphasis is placed on navigation problems rather than on speed and distance, but for those with relatively slight upper-limb handicaps the full sport is quite feasible.

Horse-riding is not suitable for all physically handicapped; but the Riding for the Disabled Association's 1974 census revealed that the 5,080 (all-age) members of its 222 member groups included some 1,659 cerebral-palsied riders and 343 with spina bifida! When medical permission is given this activity offers great excitement and challenge; for the less severely handicapped trekking offers an expedition which is an accepted part of the Duke of Edinburgh Award Scheme.

Archery is an understandably popular activity in many schools for the physically handicapped. It can be pursued by almost all children who have upper-limb mobility; indeed, it develops excellent compensatory arm and shoulder strength for those with paralysis of the lower limbs. It can easily be pursued after school (a most important factor to be borne in mind throughout), can often offer competition on equal terms with the able-bodied, and is good fun into the bargain. Once target archery has been established, a modified form of field archery, using home-made targets, can be introduced – although here safety precautions need to be even more stringent than with target archery.

Fishing, in its various forms, is man's most popular sport. It also happens to be within the capabilities of all but the most severely handicapped. Angling proper has its origins in the modest activities of pond-dipping and net-fishing, so beloved of most children. Let them graduate to rod and reel and they have an activity that is cheap, has excellent links with intellectual pursuits, combines well with camping, and may last a lifetime. Target-casting can be practised away from water, and is quite a challenging activity in itself. Access to water can be a problem, of course, particularly for those in wheelchairs. In the school at which I taught, a section of the bank of the school stream was specially prepared to accommodate wheelchair fishing; and, following the Chronically Sick and Disabled Persons' Act of 1970, local authorities are obliged to look more carefully at the whole question of access, so access to rivers may gradually become a reality for the handicapped. Children with restricting handicaps require able-bodied assistance from time to time, for instance with the landing of fish, but for fully ambulant children the fishing/camping trip provides an excellent expedition largely free of adult supervision.

Adventure on wheels

Where conditions allow, cycling has much to recommend it. Routes can be graded to suit children who are able-limbed but who have a low tolerance to exercise (e.g. asthmatics and certain cardiac conditions), and the nature of the activity allows these children to simply stop pedalling and dismount should there be a hint of distress. For the rather more severely handicapped, tricycles offer the opportunity to explore the local environment with a degree of control and stability that two wheels might not permit. Cycling can be, for some, another possible 'activity for a lifetime'; both at school and afterwards, strong links with camping, fishing and intellectual pursuits may be established. It is a permitted expedition mode for the Duke of Edinburgh Award Scheme.

Within the school environment, activities like roller-skating and trolley-riding etc. may be encouraged if sufficient hard, smooth surfaces permit. Ski-joring may be impossible in this country, but to be towed on roller skates behind a cycle could provide an exciting alternative for some! Even the prosaic wheelchair can be used in challenging situations if a little imagination is used in the design of obstacle courses and 'slalom' events. Wheelchair rambles and expeditions are also possible. I had two paraplegics who completed the full 24 km of the Duke of Edinburgh Award Scheme, 'Expedition' requirement (bronze), using a combination of wheelchair propulsion and walking with the aid of elbow crutches. With their crutches and emergency gear strapped to their chairs, they propelled themselves to a pre-arranged grid-reference point where they dismounted and continued on foot. Unseen, I motored behind them, picking up their chairs and transporting them to the next reference point, where I left them folded on the grass verge at the side of the road. The expedition continued in this way, with short walking spells alternating with longer sessions in the wheelchairs; and the route was so planned that, apart from a lunch-time rendezvous, they caught not a glimpse of me all day – although I was never more than a mile or so away! The expedition took two days, and en route the boys called at local farms and conducted a land utilisation survey. At the end of the first day, I transported them from the flat expedition area in the Vale of Pickering to a moorland campsite to the north. Thus, overnight at least, they even experienced a taste of remote upland terrain. It was the boys themselves who imposed these high standards upon their performance.

Adventure in the snow

Good snow conditions are so rare (in Britain) normally that, when they do exist, every opportunity should be taken to use them to full advantage. Skiing is a possibility but the cost of skis and the time it takes to become proficient makes it a minority sport. However there are many exciting alternatives. Gentle slopes with safe runouts offer not only the thrill of sledging and tobogganing, but also experience of less sophisticated (but, for some, just as enjoyable and challenging) activities like tray-riding and polybagging. (In the latter, exciting descents are made in padded 500-gauge polythene bags. These are cheaper and more readily produced than sledges and toboggans, and there are no hard or sharp edges to knock against – and no problems of falling off!) With the assistance of ambulant 'huskies', even severely handicapped children can experience a modest sledge tour which, in the imagination, can be a rare adventure. In all of these activities, of course, the effect of cold on immobile limbs must be remembered, and children must be suitably dressed.

Adventure going up and down

Rock-climbing and caving have a limited appeal. The Honorary Secretary of the National Caving Association reminds us that 'many able-bodied people are quite unable to go caving because of the psychological effects of the darkness and the feeling of being closed in'; and for this reason – in addition to obvious physical considerations – caving could not be recommended for the vast majority of physically handicapped children. Selected children might perhaps be offered the experience of a tour of a suitable commercial cave; but, except for one or two, there the matter will rest. However, the very fact that the majority of able-bodied people are unable to bring themselves to go caving could be just the sort of incentive that certain lightly handicapped individuals need to get involved in the activity! And if a need exists, then I believe that efforts should be made to try and satisfy that need – providing, of course, that this is realistic in terms of physical and psycho-emotional capabilities and available expertise and facilities. The same applies to rock-climbing and indeed to any other 'minority' activity.

Adventure in camp

Camping deserves special mention because of its importance as an end in itself, and as a means to an end. As an end in itself, it can offer enjoyment, excitement and adventure to almost every child. Its play origins lie in activities like shelter- and den-building, and in cooking and eating out-of-doors – all of which may be encouraged as valuable educational experiences before even a metre of tent cloth is purchased. Much has been written about camping (including a DES pamphlet, No. 58) and there is little doubt about its advantages for almost all children. But it is perhaps its great potential for social development that recommends it for use with the handicapped in general, and to certain handicaps (e.g. epilepsy) in particular.

For many children, camping in the school grounds (or, for the very severely handicapped, living in chalets at an organised camp) will be the limit of their participation. Yet this apparently modest experience can provide as much adventure for some children as wilderness camping can for others. The less severely handicapped may have the opportunity to live out-of-doors for several days while engaged on some hobby or expedition, although even here the great adventure often lies as much in one's mode of living as in the pursuit of the primary activity.

General organisation

In order to offer the type of content outlined above, a number of considerations have to be borne in mind. Some of the most important are listed below:

1. A great deal of adult assistance for supervision and general help is required. Senior able-limbed children or senior pupils from local secondary schools can be paired with the non-ambulant, for example in double canoes or tent groups.
2. Skilled help in specific areas is also needed from time to time and the need to make local contacts has already been emphasised.
3. Medical clearance is always required. One hopes this will be part of the close liaison which should exist in schools for the physically handicapped between physical educationalists, physiotherapists and the medical officer. Teachers working with a few or even one handicapped child in mainstream education must seek close collaboration with the school medical officer of health, especially for all 'risk' activities and excursions away from school.
4. Parental consent and Local Education Authority permission must be obtained. Most LEAs have their own regulations covering outdoor pursuits.
5. Safety precautions particular to a given activity, e.g. archery or canoeing, must be stringently observed. As far as possible every hazard must be identified and precautions devised.
6. Sometimes it may be advantageous to organise homogeneous groups (e.g. a wheelchair ramble, an 'expedition day' for the severely handicapped, orienteering for asthmatics etc.) but on other occasions heterogeneous groups may help the organisation run more smoothly (e.g. target archery, canoe doubles etc.). However, the *principle of mutual benefit* should always apply.
7. A good relationship with local secondary schools may enable selected children to become involved in activities that otherwise could not be catered for.

Conclusion

All who work with handicapped children must surely share three broad aims: to teach them how to live with their disabilities, how to live with others and how to help others to learn to live with them. Along with the great variety of other experiences we offer, a good outdoor pursuits programme can play a significant part in realising these aims. It will also offer the physically handicapped a place on the adventure spectrum. A very modest place, perhaps, but then, as Anderson notes in *The Ulysses Factor*,

It may even be enough to feel that you have understood, perhaps momentarily, why men *want* to climb mountains or to cross oceans in small boats. There are many kinds of window to the room of the human spirit. All that matters is that a man should be able to open *some* window.

6 Special considerations for teaching physical education to children with impaired hearing

NORA WILKINSON

The nature of the handicap

The classification of hearing-impaired children into three main categories is based on the educational expectations of children's ability to acquire language naturally. The major problem facing all hearing-impaired children and their teachers is one of communication. The more severe the hearing loss, the greater the linguistic retardation, and the more daunting the problems of communication.

1. Hard-of-hearing children depend for communication on aided hearing, and gain some help from lip-reading. 'Hearing people' are in a comparable situation in noisy surroundings such as an underground train, when they are trying to follow a conversation. They, too, unconsciously rely on a certain amount of lip-reading, and can be observed watching speakers' faces with close attention. They are familiar with the language, can fill in gaps because of their knowledge and experience, and can foresee the likely patterns of phraseology. Most hard-of-hearing children are satisfactorily placed in the main stream of education. They attend ordinary schools and receive periodic specialist help and check-ups. As a rule they wear post-aural hearing-aids, i.e. small, fairly unobtrusive aids worn behind the ear. Though their speech may be slightly defective it is usually perfectly intelligible. They benefit from favourable positioning in a formal teaching situation, and their attention needs to be caught by speakers in informal situations, so that they can help themselves by looking as well as listening.

2. Partially hearing children depend for communication on a combination of attentive listening and lip-reading. Their hearing loss is more severe than that of hard-of-hearing children, and their difficulties in verbal communication are relatively greater. Their reception of speech can be compared with that on a very poor telephone line. They are not always able to fill in the gaps by guesswork, based on experience, because their telephone line has always been poor, their experience of language consequently narrowed, and their learning probably retarded. Nevertheless they can follow ordinary educational programmes and learn verbal language through aided hearing and lip-reading, though at a rate slower than normal-hearing children, provided that they have adequate hearing-aids, a certain amount of supportive one-to-one teaching, and some specialist help.

This group of children may be placed in ordinary schools, special units attached to ordinary schools, or special schools. Children attending special units are frequently absorbed or 'integrated' into the main stream for subjects such as art, craft and physical education.

Partially hearing children may be equipped with either post-aural or body-worn hearing-aids, according to cause, nature and severity of their hearing loss. They tend to dislike their aids, particularly on cosmetic grounds, and need continual encouragement to make use of them. Particularly during their early years at school there are likely to be problems in speech and comprehension.

3. Severely and profoundly deaf children are pre-lingually deaf. They are either born deaf, or have become deaf in very early infancy before they have acquired language. They depend for communication on lip-reading, supported by aided residual hearing, and frequently use manual gestures or signs. They usually attend special schools, occasionally special units attached to ordinary schools, and only very rarely ordinary schools. They use body-worn hearing-aids. Their speech is in many cases unintelligible in their early years, and remains defective throughout their lives. The task of learning language, of comprehending and using it, is for these children a very difficult and laborious one, demanding direct one-to-one teaching over an extended period. The purposes of verbal communication are not perceived by severely deaf children until their own competence has begun to be established by skilful teaching. As a result they are usually educationally retarded and, because they miss opportunities to play and work in a group, they are usually also socially retarded.

Movement and communication

The isolating nature of the handicap of deafness makes it imperative that special attention be paid to the social aspect of education, in which linguistic competence must inevitably play an important part. The contribution of movement, dance, drama, games and athletics can be invaluable in this respect. There is some evidence that non-verbal communication, the 'body language' of movement, not only advances the child's conceptual thinking through experience and activity but may also lead to greater competence in verbal communication. For example, ideas related to space become meaningful when experienced practically in movement.

Not all thinking is verbally based and not all communication relies on words. The 'Theatre of the Deaf', which many hearing people have found intensely moving, demonstrates the richness of non-verbal communication. While the development of language is central to the education of hearing-impaired children, it would be very foolish indeed to ignore the contribution which movement can make to their intellectual, social and emotional development. The following account is by a teacher, of three months' work with a group of deaf infants whose linguistic disabilities were very severe.

We started off after we'd been in the woods collecting autumn leaves. Two of the children pretended to chop down a tree, but their actions were so cramped and inadequate that they couldn't have cut down a cornstalk. So I took back the idea into movement and we all chopped down non-existent trees with imaginary heavy axes. The children just copied me and each other at the beginning. I used some pictures to help, and a little film, and I talked all the time about what we were doing. Some of the children began to pick up a few of my phrases and repeated them. Then two of the boys decided they'd have a two-handed saw. Somebody else said 'that tree too small', and went about searching for a more satisfactory one. Once they had started thinking about what they were doing we could go on. We collected sticks to make a fire, lost the matches, burnt our fingers, found we couldn't light a fire without paper, discovered how warm it was and how much more fun it was in the dark. We used no props at any time, and as the children's language and vocabulary was so limited I am sure that their enjoyment and understanding came entirely through movement which led them on to different ideas. I told them to 'mind the sparks', and it was a long time before they really understood the lightness and impermanence of sparks. Then we moved on to bonfires and fireworks and Guy Fawkes, and it was then that one child related the imaginary explosive falling of a rocket to 'sparks'. Another was sorry for the Guy. 'Poor man', she said, 'why poor man?' It was very interesting when immediately afterwards one little boy said 'My dog frightened fireworks'.

So I think the children learnt a good deal more than they might have done just with language lessons. They began to introduce their own different individual interpretations in movement, which were extended and developed in physical communication with each other. They began to look at fires and bonfires and fireworks from the point of view of other people and animals. Their paintings were vivid and quite carefully executed. They asked for modifications of colours and were quite ready to experiment for themselves. They preferred to construct in 3D rather than to paint, though they introduced colour into their constructions and began to notice how light and positioning could affect it. They used, in other situations, phrases and idioms, and especially verbs and adverbs, which they had met in these movement lessons, and they seemed to remember the rhythm of the phrases fairly easily. Their physical movement became more spacious and more controlled in some cases, and I noticed that several of them became engaged in a kind of 'movement-dialogue' with each other . . . We never did get round to our leaf-prints, though! Their interest seemed more important.

This extract shows how verbal expression may be developed through movement. Earlier chapters have shown similar ways of linking movement and language when working with other groups of handicapped children. Though movement and dance are concerned primarily with the interpretation of ideas non-verbally, they are enriched by the stimulus of verbal skills and the 'internalised' language of thought and judgement. It is essential, for example, that children should know the names of the parts of their bodies, of the materials and equipment they use, and of the areas of space in which they move. They need to be familiar with the vocabulary of different movements and activities, the adjectives and adverbs describing them, the prepositions attached to them, and the vocabulary of comparison, similarities and differences. Both within and apart from physical education lessons, the experience and exploration of movement can provide a motive and a purpose for learning, and can make language live.

Organisation of classes

Deaf children have to rely for learning on their eyes. This may appear a self-evident statement, but it presents practical problems, and there are many occasions when teachers need to remind themselves of its importance. These children need to *see* in order to communicate. They have to *see*, to understand, and to supplement their understanding by guessing. They need to *see*, to lip-read a speaker; whether the speaker is the teacher or another child, the attention of a deaf child has to be caught and carefully directed if he is to benefit from instruction or comment. No real communication can take place in situations where this is not organised.

When talking to groups it is essential that all the children are in a position where they can see, and if possible hear, what is being said. Because running commentaries such as one would sometimes engage in with a hearing class will pass by deaf children there must be more occasions when they have to stop working in order to attend to comments and suggestions. Even when talking to an individual it is necessary to interrupt his activity.

The following extract (included by courtesy of the editor of *Talk*) may give some idea of the problems facing an intelligent hearing-impaired child in a regular school.

I've been deaf from birth and, after not too bad a time in Primary School I'm now struggling along in Middle School. This school is huge and has three floors. Complete sides of most classrooms are made of glass which give bad hearing conditions for people like me.

We have a large gymnasium with a lot of equipment, but the trouble is, when we run round it the whole gym vibrates and makes a terrific noise and when the teacher speaks I never hear her and I just carry on with what I'm doing until I notice that other children are doing something different.

In the playground at the end of playtime, the teachers often give out orders, or have something to say, but I don't hear a thing that's being said. All I hear is a mumble and all I see is the teachers' mouths opening and closing some distance away. Even worse than not hearing the teachers in the playground is the fact that amidst all the commotion of children running about shouting, I can't even make out what my friends are saying.

Situations like this require skilful teaching. Because physical education is essentially a 'practical subject' it does not mean that there are fewer problems than in the classroom. The teacher must strive to adapt the normal teaching procedures so that all may work together. Teachers need to find ways of explaining, of producing analogies and comparisons within the handicapped child's experience.

Hearing children in the group must learn to express themselves more succinctly, to demonstrate with greater clarity and control and be helped in perceiving and resolving the difficulties of their deaf companion. This can be to the benefit of all.

While teachers in ordinary schools are unlikely to have more than a very few hearing-impaired children in their physical education class, they must nevertheless play their part in aiding their total education. This points to the importance of co-operating closely with the teacher in charge of the unit or special class.

Dance and rhythmic activities

In all work on dance, rhythmic training and experience in kinaesthetic perception are very helpful to hearing-impaired children. Practice in the interpretation of musical rhythms in movement, and performance on musical instruments with reeds or vibrating skins, is exceptionally rewarding. The playing of wind instruments such as alto melodicas has been found very valuable for deaf children, and can improve both the strength and flow of their movement and the quality of their breathing. Shallow breathing is characteristic of severely deaf children. The incorporation of such auditory training in response and expression can add a new dimension to movement and drama.

Hearing-impaired children often find it difficult to conform to the arbitrary rhythms of set dances, though a metronomic beat and a long period of rhythmic training can produce rewarding results in children of middle-school age. In the primary age-groups, it is often difficult for deaf children to achieve relaxed movement while depending on visual cues, and more individualised rhythmic interpretation is of greater value in the early years. Even this can become stereotyped and repetitive unless it is continually modified and taken further by the teacher's suggestions. Talking, commenting, questioning; demonstration skilfully interpolated; pictorial and sometimes written references; the introduction of themes, dramatic situations, stories, problems, impersonations; all can be valuable aids to understanding. Children's work can be enriched by the resources of art, creative craft, music, videotape recording, and individual, paired and group role-playing.

One of the side-effects of impaired hearing is an insecurity which makes children tend to cluster. In addition, particularly in the case of more severely deaf children, spatial awareness is impaired and this carries with it some degree of clumsiness. Children who are unable to hear what is going on outside their range of vision are more likely to collide with each other and indeed with inanimate objects, and to stumble over obstacles, particularly when turning, changing direction or moving sideways or backwards. Attention must be paid to these difficulties of judgement, which can be completely eliminated by careful teaching over a period of time. Such teaching can involve imaginative games and role-playing, in which the skills of controlled movement can be practised and spatial awareness can be developed.

Games and individual sport

In these activities, the ideas of combining, co-operating, giving way, persevering and contributing as an individual to a group are all socially based, and can profitably be absorbed by deaf children on their own or in company with their hearing peers. In games there should be no problem beyond the possibility of delayed response to signals. One must be prepared for occasions when a child in a football game, unaware of the whistle, goes on triumphantly and cheerfully to shoot an inappropriate goal, but the problem is easily remedied if tolerance and a sense of humour are brought into play. In individual sports and athletic events, physically able deaf children can, of course, excel. A few adaptations are necessary. Starting signals should be visible as well as audible. In swimming it is important in the early stages for the teacher to remain alert to potential danger. Hearing-aids are out of the question, and water often blurs vision. (For more details about swimming see Chapter 8.) Similarly, deaf children cannot easily be talked up a mock rock-climb, though they can be taught to observe prearranged signals and to look for instruction. The general principle of teaching children to be alert to visual signals if they are likely to be out of touch with audible ones holds in all training in sport and team games, and the overall principle of equipping children to be finally independent and self-reliant, holds in all aspects of physical education.

The potential ability of hearing-impaired children to take part in physical education programmes is far more important than their disabilities and shortcomings. The children themselves need to recognise and come to terms with their disabilities so that they can use their own judgement to decide what they are capable of and why. The choice is finally theirs.

It is an unrewarding practice to fragment the curriculum at any level into separate subjects; the education of the child as a whole person must be constantly borne in mind. All aspects of learning should relate to children's needs and must therefore be inter-related. If the underlying aim of education is recognised to be the development of satisfactory personalities, communication must also be recognised as the keystone in any educational programme. It has many aspects and can take many forms. Non-verbal communication in physical education can not only advance verbal communication but can contribute to the growth of the child as a person. The possibilities of developing more satisfactory social personalities in deaf children by this means are only just beginning to be recognised. It is a field in which exploration and controlled experiment is likely to be most rewarding.

7 Special considerations for teaching physical education to children with impaired sight

DAVID WOOD

Normally a child with a visual acuity of between 3/60 and 6/60 on the Snellen Chart will be educated in a school for the partially sighted, while a child whose vision is below 3/60 will normally be in a blind school. The Snellen Chart makes use of letters graded according to size, and for which visual norms are known, so that a person with normal vision can clearly see certain letters at sixty, eighteen and six metres, for example. Against these norms is measured the acuity of the individual child.

An acuity of below 3/60 therefore means that a person has to get within three metres of the chart to see what a person with normal eyesight would see at sixty metres, and so on for the other standards. This is the basis of the classification, but there are many variations where an individual's field of vision may be reduced for some reason. In these cases the central vision may be far better than these standards, but there may be no vision to the sides (tunnel vision), above the horizontal (hemianopia), or in a certain area causing a blind spot (scotoma). Also a handicap additional to the visual loss will play a part in a child's placement.

Lack of clear sight, or its total absence, enforces a great dependence upon others, and the acceptance and understanding of guidance is fundamental to the learning processes of visually handicapped children. Trust must be explicit on both sides before confidence can emerge, and this confidence (or lack of it) is reflected in every movement a child makes. To walk with arms swinging, and head up, and with a heel-to-toe movement of the feet requires immense courage when the pathway is unseen, or not very clear. Confidence develops from the ability to do the basic movements correctly and efficiently. All teachers of the visually impaired must do as much as they can to develop this confidence, with perhaps most responsibility falling upon the teacher of physical education.

From birth the child with a visual handicap is at a severe disadvantage. The ability to assimilate data from the visual sense is either totally absent or impaired to such a degree that the infant cannot readily observe others and so learn by copying. Each movement has to be taught, and because of the lack of visual reinforcement development and progress are much slower. By school age, these children are often developmentally several years behind their sighted peers in walking, running and playing. Without the chance to play freely in the garden or street with a group, or to run down to the local playing fields and watch others, a whole area of life as a child is denied them.

For many, these chances come when they enter a special school; such schools are equipped with specialised apparatus to develop these skills safely and in a controlled manner. However, before the teacher can embark on his task there are many things he must do. The most important of all these is to study the medical history of each child and his present state of health because, although it is important for each child to use his available sight, it is most important that nothing is asked of him which may endanger that sight. For instance, a pupil with detached retinas should not be asked to lift heavy weights, or to dive into the swimming pool, or to bounce on the trampoline, because these activities require sudden effort, and could cause a permanent dislocation of the retinas resulting in a total loss of sight. Albinism, the lack of certain pigments in the skin and eyes, causes great discomfort for the sufferer if he is exposed to direct sunlight, and so for outdoor activities he must be allowed to remain covered, or have an application of barrier cream. Tunnel vision, as the name suggests, presents only a part of any scene to the child, so participation in widespread team games should be limited. Each eye complaint presents its limitation and the teacher must always be wary that he is not placing any child at risk. Consultations with the school doctor, and physiotherapist, are also essential so that the teacher forms a clear picture of each child's development.

Having studied the pupils the teacher must then check the changing areas to make sure they are safe. If all apparatus cannot be cleared from the walls of the gym, it must have its own parking space which never alters. A totally blind child finds his way by locating familiar objects and sounds along his proposed pathway. If he comes across a familiar object in an unfamiliar place he has to decide whether he has taken the wrong pathway or whether this object is in the wrong place. If this experience occurs often self-doubt will soon follow, with a resulting hesitance in his walk and his general bearing. Thus tidiness and regularity are essential in all areas. A chair, or open drawer which a person with normal vision will manoeuvre round, comes as a shock to a child relying on auditory clues. Just as a child needs to know the permanent positions of things, he needs to know the arrangement when apparatus work is to be done. The easiest way of doing this is to sit the class in a given spot and give a description of the layout relative to their position on the floor. A second method is to relate the apparatus to impressions made on the palm of the hands whilst giving a verbal description. The third method – and the one to use in preference to the former two – is to take each child around the apparatus and let him feel the relationships between the various pieces. In this way he builds up his own picture, and this will always be better than a sighted description.

Communication and directing by speech also need great thought. In our sighted world we make use in many ways of facial expressions, body language, and hand signals to supplement the spoken word. Disapproval, pleasure, pain, embarrassment can all be indicated clearly without a single word of speech. We see the face, and we get the message. This is not so for the blind, and only the better partially sighted have sufficient clarity of vision at close quarters to note these fine changes in the face. In this situation tones are far more important, for sarcasm, anger, laughter, tiredness are all reflected in the voice, whether we wish to show them or not. Precision of speech is therefore vital. When directing a pupil a phrase such as 'over there', followed by a hand signal, or 'near the line', 'just over a little', all mean nothing. Instructions must take the form of 'when John calls you, walk to his side', or 'take five steps to your right'. This takes a little more thought, but it is absolutely essential for the children to understand. Of course the pathways for these movements must be clear, and the responsibility for this rests with the teacher.

Great care must also be taken in choosing the programme. With players having little or no sight many larger team games such as football, or cricket, need to be played in a small area so that all the participants can feel involved. Further aid is provided in football by the insertion of small ball-bearings into the ball so that as it moves around it provides an auditory as well as a visual clue to its location. Playing on a tarmac surface has the same effect, the ball making a scuffing noise as it moves. Where running is concerned a child needs a continual locating element, and clapping hands provides a simple sound source. In competitive running clapping proves impractical, and so the end of the race, which would normally be a tape (and therefore of use only to the first to cross the line) is replaced by a brightly coloured tarpaulin on the ground. As the runners feel the change of surface underfoot they know the end has been reached. I will be dealing later with some specially adapted games, but these few suggestions serve to show that a varied programme, similar to that used in a sighted school, can be contemplated with a few changes. The most important of these is to add to or replace visual feedback with auditory and tactile information wherever possible. In addition the teacher must be actively involved, giving a commentary, positioning players correctly, and lending encouragement to all. In all this the responsibility for the selection of games rests with the teacher, and he must first of all study the suitability of each activity for each group that he takes. Just as walking into obstacles will erode self-confidence, so will involvement in activities which are beyond a child's ability and comprehension.

Special schools, by the very nature of their task, enjoy a pupil–teacher ratio better than the average state school. Classes for physical education vary from four to around twelve pupils, depending upon the severity of sight loss. Although this rules out the use of large-side games it means that the teacher can spend much more time getting to know the pupils as individuals, and this leads to better relationships. It also means that the teacher can spend more time insisting that tasks are completed correctly, and practised, before moving to more difficult items. The frequency and length of lessons is about the same as in normal schools, but there is much more flexibility to allow the individual to make progress at his own pace in the special school.

Some adaptations of traditional activities

At first, *archery* seems an unlikely sport for the visually impaired, but with slight adaptations it can be very enjoyable. Positioning the arrow on the bow is fairly easy and can be further aided by a loop of wire attached to the bow through which the arrow can be fired, and on which it can rest if need be. If a battery-operated bell is attached to the back of the target a locating sound can be given. Added to this the sectors of the target can be marked on their boundaries by string, and archery for the visually handicapped thus becomes a reality. The bell is sounded, the child lines up the arrow visually or aurally, and releases the arrow. The teacher tells the pupil where his arrow has landed, and so the activity develops. When all the arrows have been fired the child walks out to the target, and after locating the arrows determines his score from the number of string divisions to the edge of the target. Crossbows have been used for children unable to co-ordinate their hands enough to operate a bow.

The game of *cricket* also adapts well. It is best played on a rough but level surface (tarmac is ideal), with a football thrown underarm (so that it makes a noise as it approaches the batsman). The stumps are embedded in a large piece of wood, either to stand freely or be held lightly by a blind wicket-keeper. The bowler releases the ball on a call of 'ready' by the batsman. Runs are scored in two ways: if the batsman is totally blind, runs are calculated on the distance he hits the ball; if sighted, he runs either to a post about half-way up the wicket, or the full length. Fielders take part in the normal way. Totals can be individual or assessed as a team, depending on the number of players.

Adaptations for *straight running races* are given above, but on a circuit a child cannot be called from a stationary position. A totally blind pupil needs to have changes in direction called to him as he gets to the turn and so the person giving this information must be travelling backwards himself, at the same time keeping ahead of the runner. This is not easy and takes a lot of skill to do safely. For the better sighted a series of markers or helpers placed at strategic points can be used. In races for the totally blind, the children run one at a time against the clock to avoid confusion.

Most other events may be adapted safely. The shot-put can still be thrown and the discus can be thrown or rolled for distance. The long-jump can have a shorter run-up or even be a standing broad-jump, and the high-jump can be attempted from a standing position. The javelin is not recommended, because it is potentially so dangerous, but large darts with a single pointed end can be substituted instead.

In the gym a useful addition to standard apparatus is a *trampoline.* To start a small child off, a trampette with a hand rail can be used to develop the technique of rebound bouncing before going onto the larger bed. On the full-size apparatus safety devices can be added. The most important is a 'spotting belt', which ties round the waist of the bouncer; a rope held by the teacher passes through a support system attached to the roof and then fastens onto the waist belt. The teacher in this way is able to help the child in the bounces. If the gymnasium roof is not fitted with the correct tackle a climbing rope suspended over the centre of the bed gives a nervous child something to hold. Frame pads are a necessity. A box top at the side of the trampoline also facilitates mounting and dismounting. In the early stages the presence of the teacher on the bed at the same time as the pupil, either holding hands or just being that much nearer than floor level, can give reassurance to a nervous child.

Swimming needs no justification as an activity for anyone. Chapter 8 gives some suggestions for precautions necessary when the pupil is visually handicapped; a few additional points are given here. Around the pool there should be a slightly raised edge to give warning before the water is reached, and if this is not a design feature tiles can be added. Lane markers either down the length of the pool or across it prevent swimmers crossing each other. A hanging marker about one metre from each end indicates the approach of the hand rail. This marker can be made from plastic-coated string tied to a rope, with the end of the string just under the surface of the water. This is especially useful in the backstroke, where the hand is projected at some speed over the head. The side rails can be wrapped with soft material. If lane markers cannot be used, a pupil clapping hands or a bleeper can be used as markers. The best safety factor of all is the presence of the teacher in the water.

As far as actual teaching is concerned, this cannot be done in the usual manner from the side of the pool, because not all the class could be near enough to take advantage of demonstrations. So the teaching must either take place before entry, or be done by the teacher in the water. On the side the actual co-ordination of limbs can be explained and demonstrated on the pupil by the teacher, before the child goes off to practise on his own. In the water the same can be done but in addition the correct body position can be demonstrated. Once confidence in the teacher has been acquired, the visually handicapped child can perform as well as his sighted peers, and many such handicapped pupils have acquired national awards up to 'honours' level in personal survival skills, as well as taking part in competitive swimming.

There are a few activities which do not need any alterations. *Rowing* in a coxed boat for instance needs no vision because the cox is the only person facing the direction of travel. *Weightlifting* does not really require sight, only some guidance to the bar. In the same way *hill-walking* with a sighted guide, *camping*, *canoeing* in the front seat of a double tourer, are all possible for the pupil with little or no sight.

Traditional activities such as *educational gymnastics* and *modern dance* can both form part of a good programme. Indeed these are of particular value because they both demand and develop body awareness. Since it depends on an understanding of personal and general space and different levels, speed and weight of movement, educational gymnastics provides a system for understanding the body and its relationships to space, and this knowledge is a fundamental necessity for a person with limited vision. Not understanding the prepositions 'above', 'behind', 'near', 'far', leaves the child totally disoriented and very vulnerable. One of the major problems is that, unlike a sighted pupil, the visually handicapped child receives no visual feedback and cannot learn from copying others. He has a limited fund of movement skills on which to draw and will not readily demonstrate these for fear this small fund will be depleted by adverse comments. This can be likened to the difference between a man who has a large repertoire of jokes and the man who only knows one or two. The former will never be afraid of telling a joke because if his first one is not funny he has plenty more to draw upon. However, the latter will always fight shy of telling any jokes, because if his first one is a flop he has nothing to fall back on.

There must be considerable, careful formal teaching of basic skills before children can draw upon these to develop their own sequences. Since these children are unable to engage in forward and backward rolls, for instance, the teacher must help them develop other linking movements to create sequences which have flow.

Dance has a great deal to offer, but because it involves personal interpretation and a type of personal exposure pupils may find it difficult to let themselves go. As in every activity, total involvement of the teacher is essential. Any of the ideas suggested in Chapter 3 may be developed but, whereas with educationally retarded children gesture is of great importance, the teacher of the visually handicapped must inspire children to dance by versatile use of the voice.

With all these possible activities children with little or no sight can develop in the normal manner. One important part of their sports life has not been mentioned – that of being an administrator. Every sports meeting needs its jumping-pit stewards, tape holders, programme sellers and committee members, and most sports clubs are in need of interested non-playing members.

Despite the rich environment of the special school physical education programme, too many children drift completely away from any kind of sport once they have left school. This is true of many school leavers but it is particularly unfortunate for blind or partially sighted children because the majority of them ultimately take up sedentary occupations, and will be ferried to and from work by door-to-door transport. Wherever possible the school physical education teacher should try to make links for school leavers with adult clubs or leisure centres; beyond this, provision of opportunities for sport should be seen to be an important part of society's responsibility to blind and handicapped young people. This may be achieved through an after-care officer or the mobility officer of a local authority. However it is organised, lack of money or of social workers must not be permitted to destroy a valuable means of involvement in the life of the community.

8 Swimming for everyone

HELEN ELKINGTON

This chapter looks at swimming as an enjoyable activity for most handicapped people. It is not concerned with water therapy, which should be in the hands of specialist physiotherapists. Details of specific strokes and general teaching techniques are also outside the scope of this chapter. Readers are referred to general books on the teaching of swimming such as the author's *Swimming: A Handbook for Teachers* (Cambridge University Press, 1978) for this information.

Water-borne activity is probably the most beneficial form of exercise for sufferers from a wide range of physical and mental disabilities. It also happens that swimming is one of the most popular forms of physical recreation for the adult community generally, and thus offers opportunity for the handicapped and able-bodied to share in a common activity.

The three primary aims of swimming are survival, fitness and fun. It is an inspiration to see the enjoyment and tremendous psychological boost gained by successful individual learners, whatever their handicap. A most important general consideration is that all learners – within their capabilities – must be set a challenge. Too often the challenge is not sufficient to permit disabled people to benefit as fully as they could, both physically and psychologically, from water activities. A teacher should not fall into the common trap of putting a label on a handicapped person. It is important to look at ability rather than disability, to look beyond the handicap for individual potential.

Swimming is fun. Far too many are deprived of the pleasure because they are afraid of water, subjected to boring static exercises and outmoded teaching methods, and above all not sufficiently involved in the tasks set to overcome their fears. They cannot explore the many possibilities swimming opens to them: it can have a great effect on the development of the disabled learner; it improves and maintains circulation and muscle tone; through bodily movement the person comes to feel more secure; body awareness improves together with an awareness of others. But early experience is vital. The earlier in life an introduction is made to water skills the better.

Activity in water should be imaginative. A teacher aware of the scope of educational movement principles as a means of setting interesting and challenging demands will involve individuals in situations calling for mental and physical effort.

To find the appropriate method of teaching an assessment of an individual's needs is necessary. First a thorough knowledge of a learner's background is essential; this should include relevant information about his medical history and his level of physical, intellectual and emotional development.

The conditions for learning to swim must be suitable. The water and surrounding air must be at a comfortable temperature. There is considerable controversy over the ideal temperature of water; it is difficult to stipulate an ideal as it varies according to particular disabilities. A swimmer with a heart condition can suffer if the water is too cold or too hot. Swimmers prone to epileptic fits would be better in cool water, as prior to a fit the body temperature often rises and if the water is too warm the body heat is not so easily lost; in colder water a fit might be avoided. A spastic is better in warm water because it encourages relaxation. Of course it is very costly and time-consuming to raise and lower water temperatures, and those swimming in public baths usually manage well in water around 27 °C. (80 °F.); 28–9 °C. (82–4 °F.) is generally better. The air temperature should usually be about two degrees above the water temperature.

Adequate changing, toilet and shower facilities must exist. Access to and from the changing area and pool should also be organised. In newer swimming baths these provisions are demanded by law. A good supply of appropriate equipment is necessary; this is discussed below. The duration and form of the session should suit the individual. There should be adequate water space to experiment in. Frequent practice is important, as is recognition of the learner's progress. Understanding why a task is set will often improve motivation.

Learning is brought about by constantly providing opportunity to experiment, explore, select, clarify and improve. The learning must be made attractive and a teacher should seek to build the swimmer's independence and dignity.

Guidance can be given in three ways – visual, verbal and manual. The form of guidance selected by a teacher obviously should relate to the pupil's disability. A deaf pupil will benefit most from visual and manual guidance, with all words clearly mouthed and enunciated. A mentally handicapped pupil learns mainly by seeing and through manual assistance, but in some instances it is useful to give a basic verbal description of a skill. A blind swimmer learns mainly by verbal and manual guidance. Ideally a learner should be given an impression of the *whole* skill in order to establish a rhythm and technique of moving. This should be accompanied by basic comments on teaching points. The tendency of many teachers to overlook natural ability may result in overteaching.

A happy teacher–swimmer relationship is vital and results from a combination of hard work and the joy of success, with praise, correction and humour at the appropriate times. Confidence must be established but it is preferable that the learner does not come to rely solely on one person.

A record book of pupil progress should be kept and frequent appraisals made of the individual's achievement and future needs, so that challenge and motivation can be maintained.

There are two main methods of teaching swimming to those who are handicapped:

1. Using artificial aids to support the body in water, making immediate swimming movements possible. Aids can include rubber rings, arm bands, floats etc. Details are given in the section on equipment later in the chapter.
2. 'The Halliwick method', where *no* artificial aids are used and the pupil is supported by another person. This method has been in existence since 1949; the originators of this method, James and Phyllis McMillan, studied the means of relating human physiology and its movement to known hydrodynamic laws. Water is the medium used to assist or inhibit movement as required and so allow physical movement accompanied by mental response. The Association of Swimming Therapy instruct in The Halliwick Method.

   The philosophy of the method can be expressed in four basic phrases: (*a*) mental adjustment; (*b*) balance restoration; (*c*) inhibition; (*d*) facilitation. This is a valuable method; it is recommended that readers study this approach as well as that described below and select the method (or combination of methods) most suited to the individual situation.

Movement in water should be considered in terms of *what* the body is doing or able to do; *how* the body is moving or able to move; *where* the body is going or how the space available is being used.

The aim of the first visit to the pool should be to familiarise the learner with the environment and to encourage experiment and involvement in a range of activities. Static confidence-building exercises should be used with discretion and the emphasis placed on the physical and mental effort and adjustment to the environment. Activities should be designed to provide variety, challenge, movement and successful experience in order to overcome any fears of the unfamiliar medium.

Entry to water

Entry into the swimming pool can involve mechanical or manual aids, as well as self-assistance. A hoist is a costly piece of machinery and is not absolutely essential; it is embarrassing for the disabled swimmer to be slowly and mechanically transferred from land to water when a less complicated process is possible. Many swimming pools have a ramp, which facilitates entry from a wheelchair; the pupil may be able to walk down the slope, though slowly entering the water in this way is not the most pleasant of sensations. A strong roller towel with three or four helpers can be an admirable aid. The body can thus be completely protected against bumps and scrapes and damage to urinary bags etc. can be prevented, an important consideration for disabilities such as spina bifida and paraplegia.

The swimmer can be helped in and out of the pool by another person, as

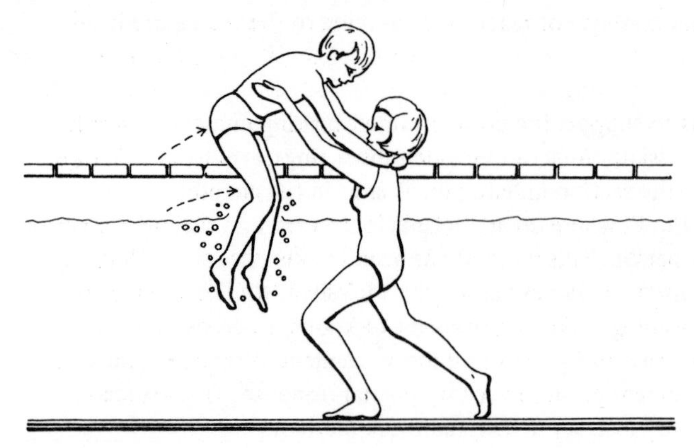

Fig. 6 Swimmer being helped in and out by another person

shown in Fig. 6. The feet of a pupil prone to spasm should *not* be placed on the rail or trough, as spasm is more likely if the feet are on a solid base.

When a swimmer can enter by the steps he should always face them during entry and exit. Whichever method is used care must be taken to avoid an unstable transition into the water.

Movement

Having successfully and safely entered the water, a learner's shoulders should be submerged. He must be able to adjust to the new element. Water upthrust can topple and tilt the body and turbulence can push and drag. The most stable position in water is the box shape, in which the knees are bent until the shoulders are under water.

Fig. 7 The box shape

Walking. The arms should be spread sideways in the water. The feet should be placed firmly on the pool bottom and can be used for movement and balance. Walking movements should be encouraged within a safe pool area; collisions with other people must be avoided and the shoulders must always be kept submerged.

Use of general space can now be taught. This means learning to move – forwards, sideways and backwards – and to turn, finally combining all four as smoothly as possible. Changing direction is demanding for the non-swimmer but an invaluable aid in gaining familiarity with the water. It is important to develop awareness of which parts of the body can lead in different directions as well.

Patterns and figures, circles, squares, triangles, figures of eight may be introduced with changes in the size of patterns. Using space and floor patterns in this way keeps the movement going, while all the time the feet are being used more effectively to give stability. Children are particularly at home with imaginative pattern-making. They love challenges, such as 'Imagine you have a black spot on the end of your nose; draw patterns with your nose in the water.' The response to this challenge is usually excellent.

The fact that water slows down movement can be used to advantage, particularly with athetoid pupils. Limb movements are slowed down and control is easier; it is possible to experiment with the speed and duration of movements as well.

Any pupil unable to walk should be supported and pulled through the water in a horizontal, usually supine position. This ensures movement after entry, and the water can stimulate the skin as the body is drawn through it, also an advantage for any pupil. This is useful as a warm-up activity.

Fig. 8 Teacher supporting and pulling pupil through water

Buoyancy

(Artificial aids can be removed at this point if the teacher is observing the pupils individually.) An appreciation of buoyancy and of the support given by water is essential. When possible pupils should experiment with the prone and supine positions and with vertical, and horizontal tucked positions. They must be taught how to regain the standing position in water straightaway.

The importance of breathing in buoyancy and indeed in all aspects of water activity must be stressed. Air in the lungs assists flotation; exhalation usually results in a loss of buoyancy. This can be particularly well illustrated in the mushroom (Fig. 10) and the horizontal supine float. Whether or not a pupil is wearing

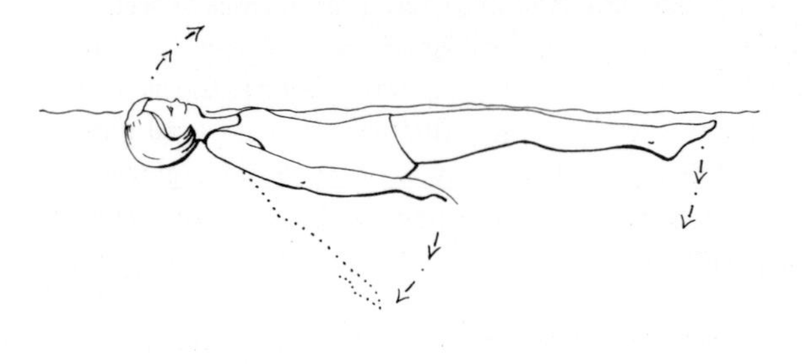

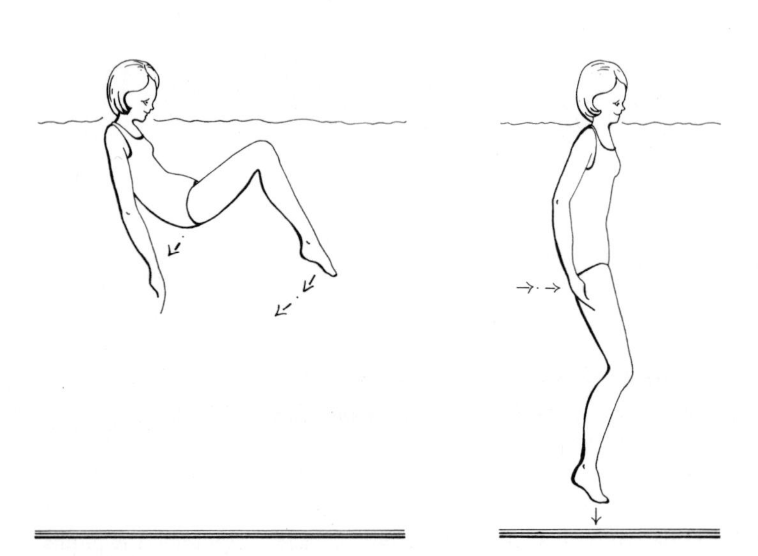

Fig. 9 Standing from supine or prone positions

buoyancy aids the ideal floating position will vary according to body build, placing of limbs, air in the lungs, and disability. Many boys and young men with little fat in the hip region find the vertical float more successful while many girls, women and older men with more fat around the hips and thighs will find a horizontal float more successful. If the arms are stretched beyond the head, increasing the amount of denser tissue at the top half of the body, the legs will rise

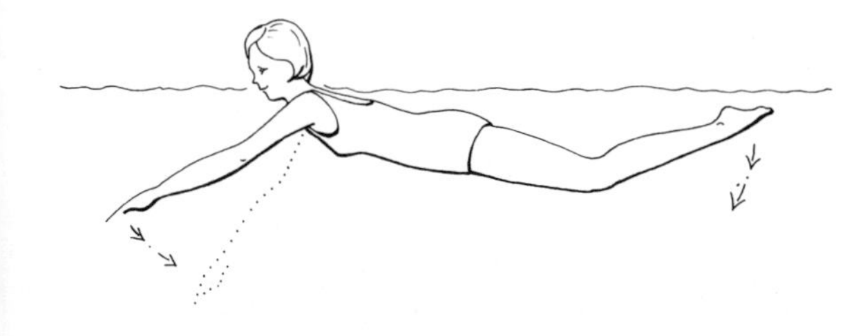

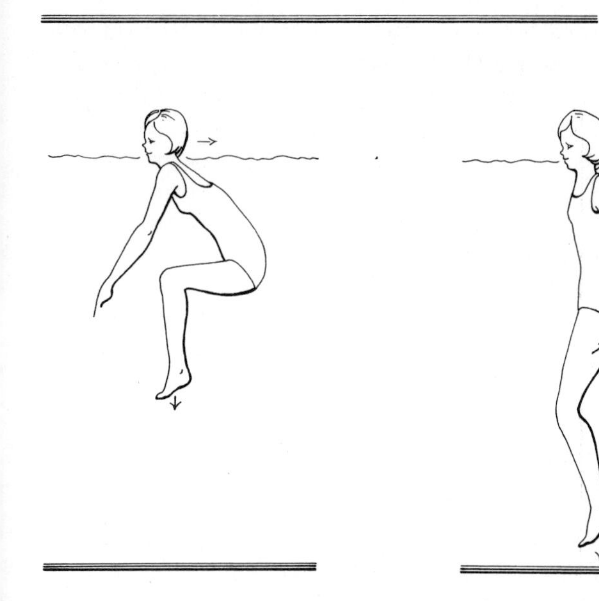

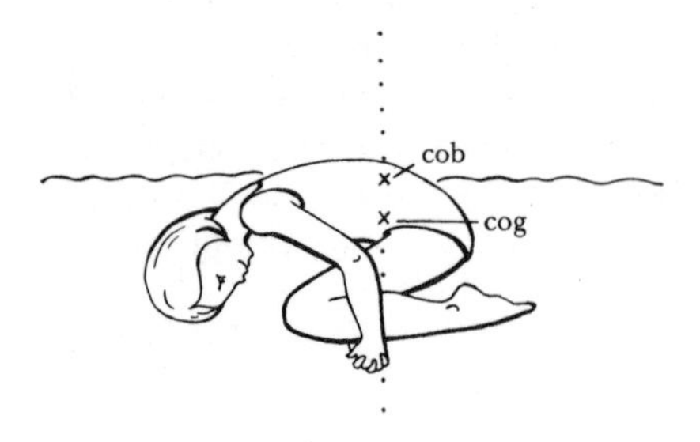

Fig. 10 The mushroom float

more easily. Paraplegics and spina bifida swimmers often find their legs ride high in the water.

In all floating positions the greater part of the body will be under the surface of the water, and swimming efforts should therefore be directed towards driving the body through and not over it.

Experiments with buoyancy

With the rubber ring and armbands on it is possible to float and experiment with body shapes. The pupil should assume the box shape. Stress the sitting position with the hips, hands and arms depressed. This may be repeated several times. Ask 'What do you feel your feet doing?' The upthrust of water will be felt and the feet will rise off the pool bottom until the learner is afloat. Water support is being experienced.

The exploration of body shape will help to develop balance and relaxation. The three basic body shapes, star/wall, pin and ball, can be executed on the horizontal plane in the supine and prone position.

With younger learners draw upon experience and imagination; for instance, 'Imagine it is a very hot day and you are going to sunbathe on the surface of the water.' Some children choose the prone position, others the supine. All children should be asked eventually to try both and to remember the value of breath control. 'Alter your head and arm position; what difference does it make to your body in water?' Children can experiment and will be able to give the answer rapidly.

From the prone or supine floating positions the appreciation of balance and alteration of body shape can be developed by simple suggestions. 'Make yourself as wide as you can to get really hot.' 'The sun is going behind a cloud and it is

Fig. 11 The three basic body shapes

getting colder.' Eventually the challenge may be given of moving from one shape to another without putting the feet down. The speed at which this change of shape is brought about should be considered; a slower, more controlled transition will help the body to maintain balance.

Propulsion (with aids, initially)

An opportunity for the learner to propel his body in a horizontal position should be given as soon as possible. When this is achieved the gain in motivation is tremendous.

To propel the body forward through the water a force must obviously be exerted backwards. In order to produce forward movement the correct hand and arm thrust is vital. A swimmer must be aware that 'for every action there is an equal and opposite reaction'; an over-water, wide swinging-arm recovery causes the hips to swing laterally, and a strong leg-kick is required to stabilise them; if the arms press down the body rises. It is also important to 'fix' the hand during the arm movement to eliminate 'slip' as much as possible.

A swimmer must be helped to find the most efficient body position in the water. A horizontal position creates least resistance to water. Too much lift of the head is likely to cause the legs to sink and creates drag.

Before beginning swimming strokes, the learner should be able to make use of the rail or trough for resting. A thalidomide pupil minus arms, but with full use of the legs, can use a foot hooked under the rail, while a lower-limb amputee has no problem in using his arms or head for support.

The strokes

Most beginners can cope best in the supine position. Initially a semi-sitting position often helps pupils with very high hips, such as spina bifida or paraplegic children.

Leg action

The leg action is generally considered essential for balancing the body during the whole stroke. If the ankles are flexible effective propulsion can be achieved as well. In many cases the legs are relied upon as the sole means of propulsion. In the prone or supine position alternating or simultaneous leg actions are possible, and both should be tried in order to discover the most suitable.

Alternating kicks on the vertical plane (the leg action of the crawl) are popular. They are initiated at the hips with the legs extended as much as possible, with ankle flexibility an advantage for a 'flipper effect' driving the water backwards. The depth of the kick will vary but little more than body depth is necessary. Too deep a kick and overbending the knees should be discouraged, as these may cause the body to travel in the opposite direction to that intended; or there may be marked hip undulation, which is unproductive.

Simultaneous kicks on the horizontal and vertical plane provide effective propulsion, but to be really successful require good mobility at the hips and ankles. A breaststroke kick can be difficult if the foot cannot bend and turn outwards satisfactorily after the knees have bent in preparation for the drive backwards. A fish-like simultaneous kick such as the dolphin butterfly stroke's is invaluable and, where arms can be used, may be combined with a breaststroke arm action. This kick is initiated at the hips, with the legs kept together as much as possible. The knees bend and the lower part of the leg and ankles kick back. Continuity is an advantage in the 'dolphin butterfly', as a glide after the backward kick will encourage a hydro-planing effect.

The kicks can all be tried in the prone or supine position. They do not have to conform to any rigid swimming law. The intention is movement rather than competitive speed. Many disabled swimmers progress through water using only one leg. As soon as the individual is capable and confident, artificial aids should be removed.

Arm actions

A prone or supine horizontal floating position should be adopted. In the prone position either simultaneous rounded arm movements similar to the breaststroke or alternating dog-paddle movements can be practised. The athetoid pupil or anyone with co-ordination problems is usually better with a simultaneous type of movement concentrating initially on either arms or legs only.

In the supine position the arms can be simultaneously swept sideways from the thighs, palms facing downwards. They are rotated when a line level with the shoulders is reached. This faces the palms of the hands towards the feet ready to sweep simultaneously towards the sides of the body.

An over-water arm recovery is not necessary to obtain propulsion. It is important at first to keep the arm movements in the water and *close* to the body, yet placed to balance it. If a swimmer using dog-paddle arm action does not extend far enough forwards prior to each pull he can overbalance. Similarly, if a breaststroke pull is too wide, passing beyond the shoulder, the swimmer will also be unbalanced.

As well as teaching the generally accepted arm strokes, the teacher can encourage the swimmer to discover movements particularly appropriate to his physique. For instance, a hemiplegic in the prone position might attempt a dog-paddle movement using one arm; if he is encouraged to use the weak side of the body as well and continue the dog-paddle movement with the able arm, a 'rolling dog-paddle' develops. The same pupil attempting the breaststroke arm action might hold the hand of the weaker arm with the able hand. The arms extend forwards together, the movement improves and an adapted breaststroke develops.

Sculling on the back is invaluable for the disabled. It involves an arm movement near the body and in the water. Because the body is supine the swimmer is able to rest his head on the water. Sculling propels, balances and controls the body. Any swimmer suffering from any disability where general weakness and loss of muscle tone are major problems should be taught this skill at the earliest stage.

The rubber ring and even arm bands can be removed when the learner's push is strong enough to achieve forward movement. The isolation of arms only at this stage illustrates the value of arms for propulsion. As the arm movement improves attention should be drawn to the importance of holding the fingers together and keeping the continuity of each cycle.

The ultimate thrill and feeling of accomplishment is surely reached when arms and legs are used together and in co-ordination. Many different variations and combinations are possible to cater for individual needs.

The Halliwick Method, mentioned earlier, uses a most effective means of assisting the pupil to move. The teacher stands in the water and creates turbulence with his hands. This causes the floating pupil to travel towards the area of turbulence. (A mother swan leads her family through water in a similar way.) The method is ideal for the severely disabled; when they see the roof of the pool pass by overhead they realise they are travelling; no one needs to hold them and the sensation is thrilling.

Breathing

Breathing is essential, obviously, but it also can interfere with the swimming stroke. Whether the pupil is walking through water, floating or swimming, correct breathing is vital. It is necessary to consider *why* there is a need to breathe, *how* to breathe and *when* to breathe.

Why. The answer would seem obvious but needs stressing, especially with beginners. Breathing is partly voluntary and partly reflex. During any effort the depth and frequency of breathing increases automatically, but in swimming breathing must be fitted into the stroke cycle so that there is sufficient time for it to be efficient. It should be realised how much water pressure affects the breathing in the prone strokes. More effort is required than in normal breathing to expand the chest cage against the water pressure outside.

How. The learner can be helped to understand how to breathe by the teacher's stressing *exhalation*, but not to the point of exhaustion. It should be controlled and of sufficient duration, so that inhalation will follow easily. If a person is swimming under pressure, for instance in a sprint, the exhalation is usually explosively forced out towards the last part of the underwater arm stroke. In leisurely exercise the exhalation can start a little sooner in relation to the underwater arm stroke, and air should be exhaled slowly, to be followed by adequate inhalation. Exhalation should be mainly through the mouth.

When. The timing of explosive breathing in swimming strokes follows the same basic rule; that is to say, in all strokes it can be related to the arm stroke. Exhalation should start *after* the main part of the propulsive effort of the underwater stroke and continue until the mouth has cleared the water, to be followed naturally by inhalation. In leisurely swimming, the exhalation phase can be over a longer period of the underwater arm stroke. Trickle breathing, as it is called, is often more desirable for the disabled initially, as they are generally able to cope at this less exhausting pace with the longer phase of breathing out and in.

Many pupils 'drink' water and the mentally handicapped, particularly, tend to do this; any pupil with a speech defect might also find breathing a major problem. Such children should be taught to *blow out* whenever their faces meet the water.

In the very early stages of swimming, children can be encouraged to breathe by blowing coloured balls along the water surface.

Watermanship activities

Watermanship activities provide contrast to swimming strokes and help to 'waterproof and drownproof' swimmers. They require competence in propulsion, orientation and reorientation, awareness of level and change of level, of shape and change of shape, and of direction and change of direction, and variations of speed.

Group and individual activities should be encouraged at the appropriate stage. Group activity in particular does much to encourage the development of relationships with others; social integration is an important part of any swimming programme for disabled people.

Lessons with handicapped pupils must have plenty of variety; mentally handicapped children do need a great deal of repetition but variety is also essential for them. The ideas which follow may be used for this purpose.

Individual activities

Sculling. The body is made to travel through the water by moving the hands as paddles inwards and outwards. The elbows should be as straight as possible and the hands kept close to the body. The hands should pivot rhythmically from the wrist. Force is applied at right angles to the direction opposite to the direction of travel. Continuous pressure is desirable since it aids propulsion, smooth travel and the maintenance of a stable body position. The hand position should be constantly adjusted to maintain pressure.

Extensions of simple sculling include moving to a drum-beat head first, feet first, and on the spot, changing from one scull to another on every heavy beat. Sculling can also be performed to music which has a clear beat, such as Russ Conway's 'Side-saddle'.

Stunts. Gymnastic skills in water, often termed stunts, are enjoyed by many pupils. Basic stunts include:

(*a*) The tub. Begin with the body stationary in the supine position. The flat scull should be used. The head is steady with eyes looking upwards and the legs and feet are extended and together. The knees are drawn to the chest into the tub position and the body is revolved smoothly throughout 360° in a clockwise or anti-clockwise direction, pivoting on the seat. It is often useful to tell children to imagine they are sitting on a drawing pin.

(*b*) Somersault back tuck. From the back layout position the body rotates backwards in a ball shape as the arms sweep forwards.

(*c*) Log roll. The body is stretched out on the water surface with arms extended beyond the head. Without using the arms or legs it is then rotated on the water surface in the stretch position.

(*d*) Corkscrew. Identical to log roll but only one arm is extended. The other is by the side of the body.

These stunts can also be executed to a drum-beat and music. Paul Mauriat's

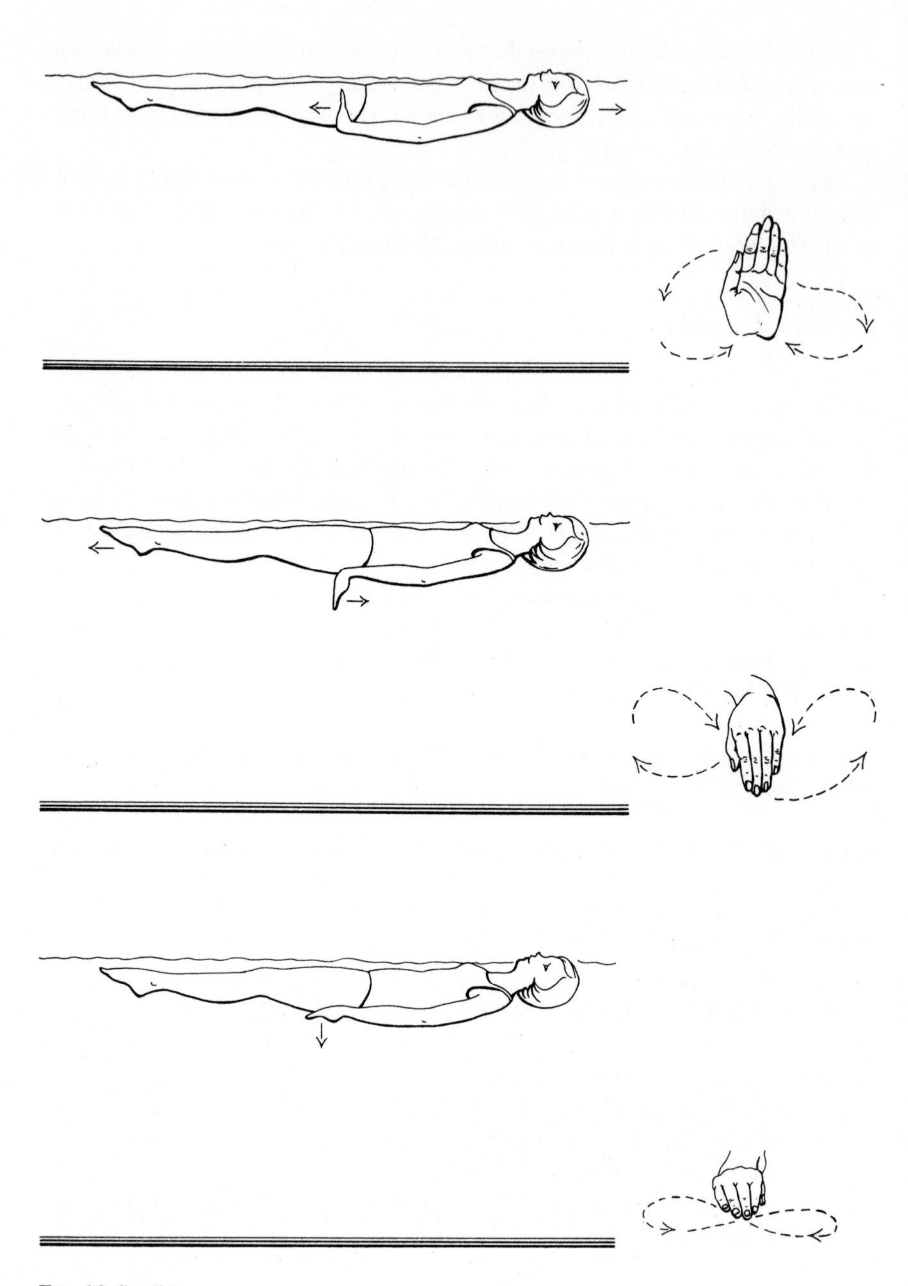

Fig. 12 Sculling

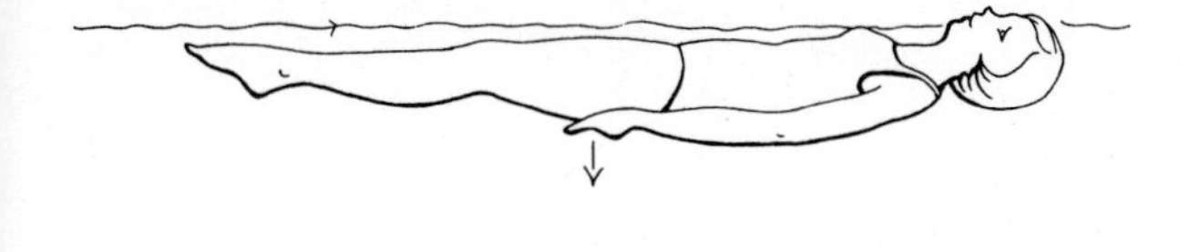

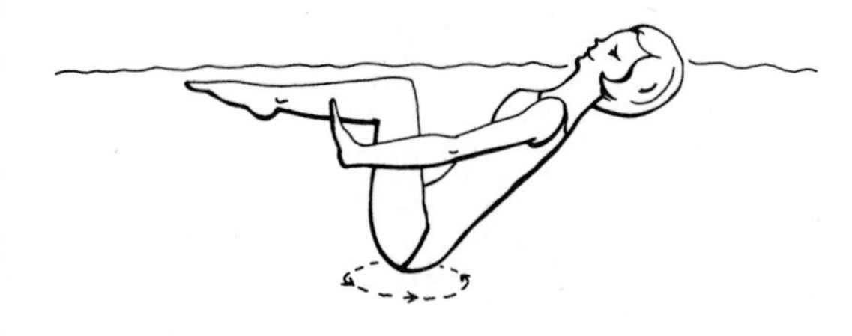

Fig. 13 The tub

'Love is blue' is ideal for a sequence of sculling and stunts. Music is great fun and adds greatly to the enjoyment of the sessions.

Weight transference. (Artificial aids should be removed for any underwater work.) Transference of body weight can be a most effective exercise. For example, children may be asked to put their body weight on to both hands, move to one hand, and then try to balance on any part of their body other than hands and feet. This causes great amusement! The upthrust of water can be felt in this activity, so speed in moving from one body position to another is an important consideration: 'Sit on the bottom going down slowly', and 'Jump into a tucked position and sit on the bottom'. The fast movement displaces water and the pupil will sit speedily on the pool bottom. Breathing out should be mentioned as an aid to sinking.

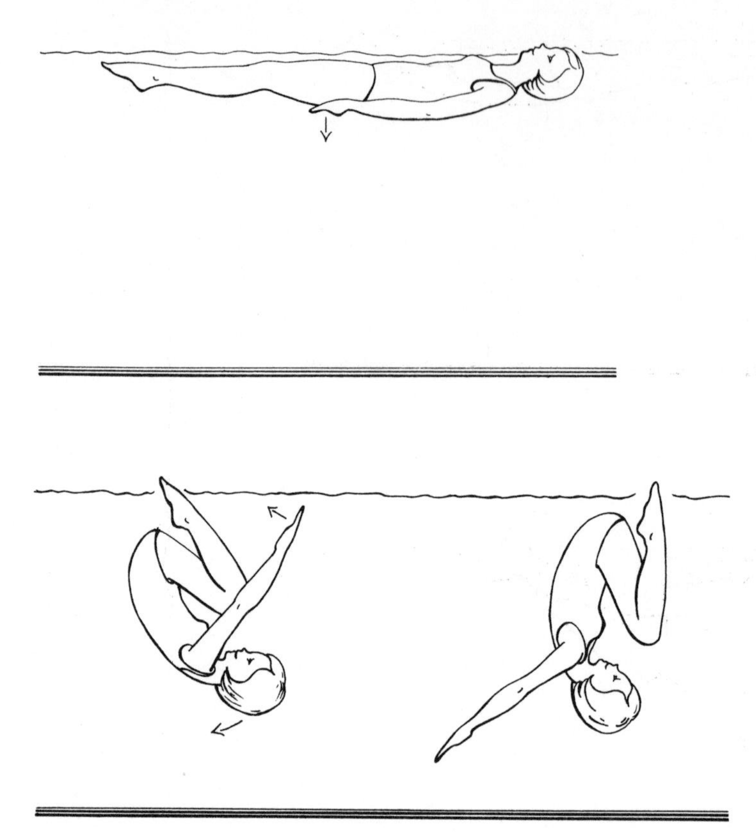

Fig. 14 The somersault back tuck

Individual activities with small apparatus. Apparatus is discussed further in the 'Equipment' section of this chapter.

Hoops are very useful for the children to swim through in as many different ways as possible, and to somersault through. Mongol children are wonderful at somersaulting and love these activities. Incidentally, Mongol children enjoy staying on the pool bottom too, so great care should be taken by the teacher to retrieve all pupils. Veronica Sherborne attributes this submerging habit to the need for security and to the fact that the pool bottom is solid and seems so secure.

Bricks (4 kg and 2 kg) can be used as objects to dive for. Coffee-jar tops are also useful sinkers and can easily be seen under water. The challenge of picking up objects helps pupils to open their eyes and to overcome fear of water.

Ropes allow pulling, pushing, weaving in and out, pendulum swinging and many other activities. Blind pupils find them an invaluable aid when they are learning the geography of the pool. If the rope is placed lengthways, a lane's

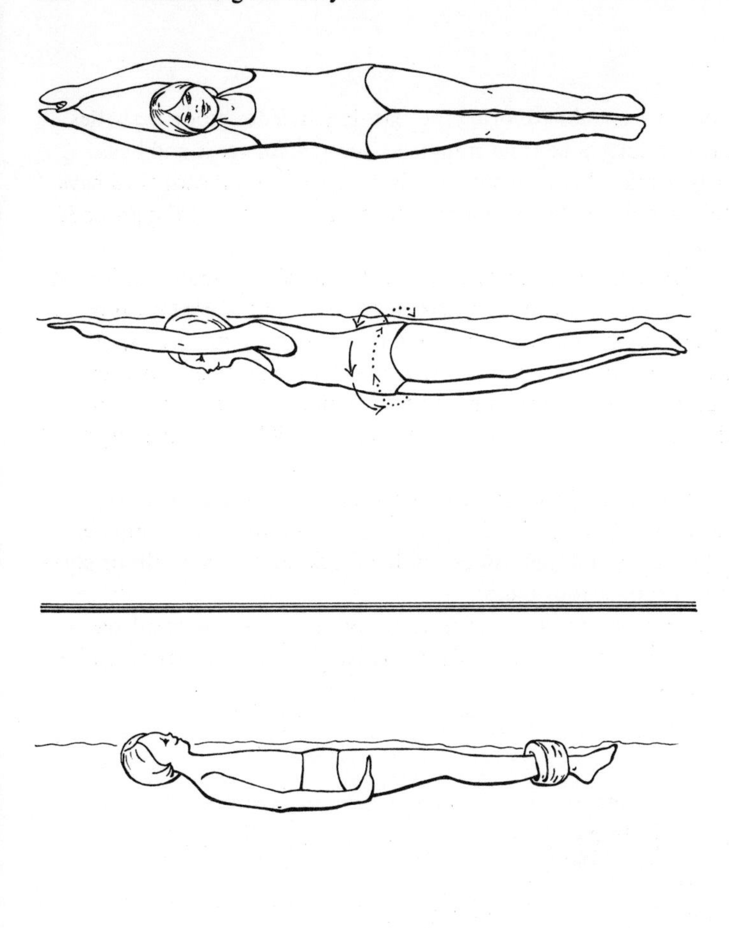

Fig. 15 The log roll. An arm band round one or both ankles can help lift the feet to the surface. This is useful with heavy-limbed pupils. It is not ideal for beginners or small children. This method must be used only under careful supervision

width from the wall, a blind pupil will learn to guide himself by sound-waves from the wall on one side and the lane rope on the other.

Buoys and other floating objects can be useful markers and obstacles to be negotiated.

Weighted skittles and *mats* can be used in the shallow end of the pool to encourage further underwater activities, such as movements on all fours on and off the mats and through and round skittles.

Group activities

It is desirable whenever possible to bring the class together for group activities. These may include holding hands and stepping sideways, forwards and back. This is particularly useful where a mental disability causes an individual to have an aversion to fellow human beings. If a song suitable to the age of the group is sung this can help the atmosphere.

It is not easy to get a group to spread out. In the Royal Commonwealth Pool (learner pool), Edinburgh, there are large coloured spots on the pool bottom. It is easy to spread the pupils out by asking them to 'Stand on a coloured spot'. Once the group is spread out various activities can be done in unison. A drum may be used to give a rhythm, with children submerging on a heavy bang, or a song like 'Baa, Baa black sheep' can be sung or played, children submerging on the word 'black'.

Music can also play a part in submerging activities. For this a good tune is 'Song of the Nairobi trio', played by the group Hot Butter on their album *Popcorn*. Still spread out, the children can lie on their backs and do log rolls or corkscrews in time to a drum-beat or music.

A ball held in one hand can be a useful aid to rotation too. The pupil keeps the arm *low* and *close* to the body and places the ball in the other hand, as illustrated.

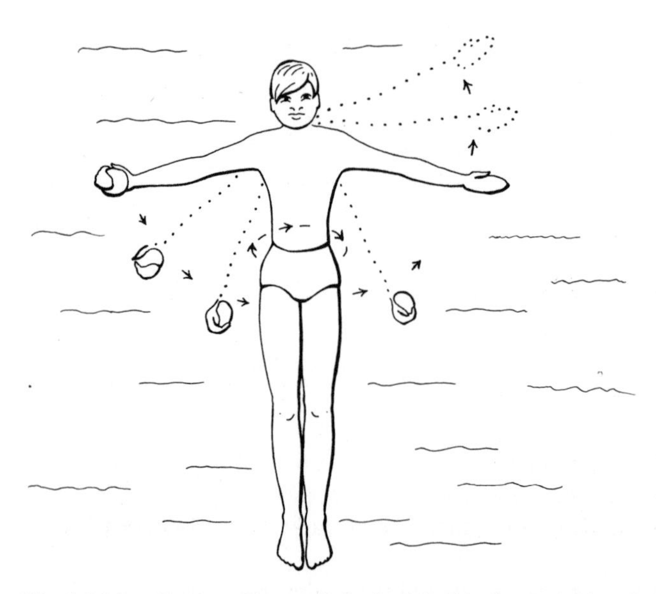

Fig. 16 Learning to roll round the longitudinal axis using a ball. The right arm remains in the water and stretches across the body to place the ball in the left hand

Special problems in swimming related to specific conditions

In all cases medical advice must be sought before swimming lessons begin. More detail of the following medical conditions is given in Chapter 4. Here detail is given in relation to the effect of these conditions on swimming.

Spastic paralysis. This disability is due to spinal cord or brain damage and results in *increased* muscle tone. The limbs are rigid and, in certain cases, if an area of the brain is damaged there may also be uncoordinated muscle contractions in various parts of the body (athetosis). The swimmer may be affected on one side of the body (hemiplegia), both sides (tetraplegia), or in both legs (paraplegia).

Relaxation is of prime importance for children with these disabilities. A teacher must be careful not to upset the relaxation of a weak muscle and must be aware of an individual's limit in a session. A stiff, tense body will sink and a spasm will create this effect. If a severe spastic inhales water he may have a spasm. Controlled breathing is consequently very important. Emphasis should be on exhalation and breathing should not be too deep.

Initially balance is a problem and the most suitable position must be found. Once balance has been established movement can begin. It should be remembered that the paralysed part of the body sinks more easily and that a hemiplegic, for example, will rotate and sink towards the affected side.

The swimmer should be encouraged to use the paralysed side if possible. A bilateral movement is desirable for a hemiplegic and a rolling dog-paddle or assisted breaststroke as described above are appropriate. The overarm trudgeon stroke can be useful, too, with the good arm carried over the water. Head position is important to help the swimmer keep straight.

A spastic with uncontrollable movements (the athetoid) can be difficult to teach, as the head is often thrown back, possibly sideways, or even submerges. The uncoordinated pupil is often better at moving through water using a simultaneous movement such as the inverted breaststroke.

It is usually best to introduce the spastic pupil to swimming movements in the supine position. Patience is essential. It will often take a spastic pupil a long time to complete a task.

Poliomyelitis. Fortunately, there are few young people suffering from this condition today, but the recent dramatic reduction in the number of children receiving the polio vaccine may bring an upsurge of cases.

This condition is due to the injury by disease of the 'nerve circuit' between the brain and the peripheral nerve endings in the muscles, resulting in dead or practically dead flaccid, floppy muscles. There is a *decrease* in muscle tone. A large part or small part of the body can be affected. The body will be unbalanced due to deformity from the paralysis, unequal muscle strength in various areas and poor circulation in the limbs of the severely affected. If the legs are affected the pupil should start in the *supine* position, as flaccid limbs float easily. Such pupils can be worked progressively harder, but it is especially important that they are kept warm.

Amputees. Balance is vital and head adjustment can be particularly helpful. Often leg amputees ride high in the water but usually their arms are strong from the use of crutches. A supine position is again the obvious starting position.

Spina bifida. In this condition paralysis and deformity vary in severity from slight muscle imbalance to complete paralysis of the body below the lesion, including the bladder and bowels. Paralysis may be flaccid or spastic or a combination of both. Loss of sensation to touch is common. Often the sense of passive position may be impaired and there may also be incontinence.

The pupil should be taught to use the intact muscles *above* the level of lesion and any residual muscle power below it. Manual guidance of the leg-kick is often valuable. It is useful to start with a supine, semi-sitting position; pupils with spina bifida also ride high in the water if their legs are flaccid. If there is a loss of sensation great care should be taken to avoid damaging limbs by scrapes and cuts; ulcers can develop and take a long time to heal. The medical certificate should say if the child is fitted with a Holter valve (see Chapter 4). This must be checked, and great care taken to avoid knocking the valve in any way during the swimming lesson.

Paraplegia. This is the result of damage to the spinal cord by disease or trauma and paralysis may be flaccid or spastic or a combination. The extent of the paralysis depends on the level of the lesion in the spinal cord. A tetraplegic should start in the supine position as paralysed arms are difficult to lift. Breathing without the support of the arms to lift the head fractionally is a further problem if the prone position is used. Care should again be taken to avoid damage to the skin.

Muscular dystrophy. Boys only are affected by this, generally speaking. It is a progressive disability producing flaccid limbs, weakness and loss of tone in all muscles, including those involved with respiration. Head control and breathing must be carefully watched and fatigue must be avoided. Initially the supine position and sculling movements, which do not use too much energy, should be used.

Multiple sclerosis. This usually affects young adults. There are remission waves, periods when the pupil appears to be fit for months or even years, and during them swimming is advantageous. Symptoms may vary and may be scattered through the body. There may be increased muscle tone – spasticity and rigidity

– or a decrease in muscle tone with incontinence, disturbed vision, loss of balance and sensation.

It is important to avoid fatigue and to remember that shivering may be due not to cold but to fatigue. The tired pupil should get out of the pool immediately. In some severe cases a therapy pool might be preferable to a normal swimming pool. All swimming movements should be designed to conserve energy; sculling, dog-paddle and breaststroke are ideal in this respect.

Thalidomide damage. Because of a drug taken by the child's mother during pregnancy, all or part of one or more limbs will be missing. The remaining limbs can be exercised and are usually strong.

Once again, a supine position is desirable in the initial stages, particularly if the arms are affected. The swimming style used will obviously depend on which limb or limbs are affected. A secure balanced position must be found which will compensate for any tendency to roll.

Haemophilia. The haemophiliac is affected by a disease transmitted by women and affecting men. Haemorrhages, particularly internal haemorrhages, are the main danger, so swimming must be controlled to avoid sudden movements and knocks. Either the prone or supine swimming position may be adopted.

Orthopaedics. Orthopaedic cases may have a temporary or permanent disability. They are often fit and strong but may well lack flexibility; however, they are usually keen and able to adapt where necessary to water.

Rheumatoid arthritis. This is a generalised disease which can be very painful. There may be stiffness and deformity in the joints affected. It is essential to keep the swimmer warm and to avoid fatigue. A supine stroke will not tire the swimmer as much as a prone stroke in which head control and breathing can be difficult.

Epilepsy. In between attacks epileptics are often quite fit. There is considerable controversy over whether or not epileptics should be allowed to swim. Generally it is felt that they *should* swim in organised sessions where their condition is known and they can be closely watched.

It is essential to have sufficient helpers on the side of the pool so that a swimmer can be reached and removed from the water immediately if a fit occurs.

Impaired hearing. Hearing-impaired children and adults can cope well with swimming and can be taught a great deal. Lack of balance may be an initial problem but can be overcome.

Problems of communication are dealt with in Chapter 6, but in a swimming pool one must be able to spot pupils if they move out of their safety area; coloured hats should be worn for easy identification.

Impaired sight. Would-be swimmers in this group should have medical clearance before entering chlorinated water. Other swimmers should be warned that there are unsighted pupils in the pool. There should be helpers on the bath side to protect blind swimmers from knocking themselves against the wall. Again, coloured hats are useful for identification.

The main problem is orientation. The geography of the pool – the depth, width and length, entry and exit points, rails and troughs – must be appreciated. A comprehensive 'brain picture' can be built up by counting out walking paces and working out the number of strokes to each length, then swimming strokes to a rhythm given by a handclap, drum-beat or suitable music. Instructions should be given from directly in front of the swimmers since a turn of the head often causes a change of direction. Orientation is easier in the prone position. Ropes can be helpful, as mentioned earlier.

Mental disabilities. The mentally disabled often love swimming. It is important to remember that disabilities and therefore understanding vary considerably. Guidance must be manual, visual and often very basic verbal. Repetition is important but variety too is necessary, to maintain interest and motivation. Equipment which is colourful, interesting to touch and intriguing in shape will help to stimulate interest. Discipline is as important with mentally disabled children as it is with any others. Behaviour problems must be anticipated: they tend to catch one unawares at times, and loss of control in the swimming pool can be disastrous.

Bladder control is of course desirable. But in well-chlorinated water a certain amount of incontinence is not harmful. (In a public session it is not unusual for the water to be contaminated by a certain amount of urine.) Plastic underpants help and the bladder should be emptied before swimming. Regrettably pupils lacking bowel control should not be allowed to swim. Medical advice should, of course, be sought over these problems.

Equipment

Different aids have their advantages and disadvantages but they should not, under any circumstances, be dangerous or impede movement to any extent. Aids can be adapted to individual requirements and disabilities. The main purposes are to get pupils into a swimming position and support them, and to provide objects to swim through, round, onto or to pick up. The colour, shape and texture of the objects can also create interest, particularly amongst the mentally disabled.

Rubber rings. Three sizes (16, 18 and 20 in. are available at present), can be used. A safety tape over the shoulders should be used to prevent the ring slipping downwards; a tape between the legs will prevent it from riding upwards if the pupil has no arms.

Armbands. The double- or single-chambered type can be used, and should have safety valves. For very small children thedouble-chambered arm bands can be halved.

Rubber neck-rings. These come in three sizes, and support the head. The neck ring is invaluable if the pupil lacks head control.

Floats. These come in various sizes and materials. The foam type is good if it is 2 in. (5 cm) thick, approximately 9 in. (23 cm) long and 7 in. (18 cm) wide. A large float made of strong plastic is available and is 18 in. (46 cm) in length. It is ideal for some adult pupils.

Balls, hoops, ducks, buoys, coffee-jar tops. Any intriguing object to challenge pupils both above and underwater should be used. Colour, texture and shape can be important.

Flippers. Thalidomide children find these invaluable, as do pupils requiring help with leg movements, as their main or only means of propulsion. Flippers also help to achieve a deeper or straighter kick. They are available in sizes for adults and children.

Rubber bricks. 2 kg and 4 kg bricks or coffee-jar tops can be used for retrieval from the bottom of the pool.

Courlene rope. Rope can be used to divide the pool lengthways and widthways. It can also be used to set targets for pupils: 'Swim underwater between the two ropes'.

Clock. One with a sweep second hand is useful for activities such as survival practice, speed measurements and timed endurance swims.

Drum. A clear basic rhythm can be set. It is valuable for sculling and change of direction exercises. It is ideal for use with the mentally handicapped.

Music. This can be used in many ways to stimulate movement and to create a happy, relaxed atmosphere. It should be selected to suit the pupil and activity. (See 'Watermanship' section, above, for a few ideas.)

Float suits. These can be a useful aid.

Rubber mattresses, towels etc. These are useful for entry and exit from the pool and protection on the pool side.

Weighted belt. Lead weights are placed in pockets to provide weight to lower the hips. This is a valuable aid for any pupil whose hips ride too high in the water. (The belt should be made so that the lead can be easily removed or added according to individual needs.)

Awards

All swimmers enjoy challenge and a wide range of swimming awards offer this. Handicapped swimmers can gain particular satisfaction from success in normal swimming award tests. There are also special awards for the disabled, the most satisfactory being those offering a wide choice of activities. It is important, however, that award schemes are not used as the basis of individual swimming programmes. A wide repertoire is desirable and as swimmers improve in confidence, strength and stamina they can take awards in their stride.

The club

This is a subject on its own. A swimming club requires the usual administrative officers – chairman, secretary, treasurer, transport officer, committee members. The committee should where possible involve a range of professional people such as doctors, physiotherapists, occupational therapists, remedial gymnasts, physical educationalists, nurses, social workers, local council representatives etc.

A regular register should be kept to record pupil attendance and progress. Initially the launching of the club must be well organised if the group is to attract attention. Transport, helpers on land and in water must all be completely in the picture as to their duties and methods of working.

A fund-raising group will probably be necessary. Insurance requirements must be satisfied. Bodies such as Rotary clubs and Soroptimists can give invaluable support. Galas can be held. The wide range of disabilities in some instances creates many a headache for handicappers. But the effort to give each swimmer a fair chance is extremely worth while.

To show what can be done, a team of disabled swimmers swam a relay across the English Channel and not only completed the swim but set the record for the year for the fastest team crossing – of disabled *or* able swimmers.

This chapter is intended not only to help teachers and others professionally involved with handicapped children and adults to provide stimulating and satisfying swimming lessons, but to encourage others to give of their time to help many more disabled people to enjoy the sport. The effort involved is minimal, the satisfaction great.

9 Some methods of integrating handicapped children into physical education and recreation with other young people

DOUGLAS WILLIAMSON

Integration and handicapped pupils

There is a great danger that any member of society who deviates from the norm in physical appearance or who shows an unusual behaviour pattern may become isolated and segregated. Perhaps the most important concern in work with handicapped children is that they should be offered the chance to live as normal a life as possible as full members of the community.

The Warnock Report (1978) gives clear direction for much greater integration of handicapped pupils into normal schools, but it is unlikely that money will be available for the necessary alterations to school buildings and for additional human resources in the immediate future. It is necessary for teachers and pupils within the present pattern of segregation in education to seek other ways of overcoming the problem.

For the purpose of this chapter, integration is considered in three contexts: special schools, special units attached to primary and secondary schools, and handicapped pupils in the mainstream school systems. Physical education is an excellent medium for promoting integration for it offers many opportunities for group play while at school and for post-school recreation.

The degree of integration which may be achieved will vary. At one extreme there is the pupil isolated in a hospital school, perhaps out in the country, at another the handicapped youngster who is an accepted and participating member of a regular school class. One cannot expect 'integration' to be fully successful for all handicapped youngsters. Some pupils lack the physical capacities, social ability or maturity and are thus severely restricted. Yet if teachers are optimistic and provide opportunities they are often surprised by the results.

Integration can be considered as a three-stage process:

Contact	Involvement	Interaction
(coming together)	(a formal game or activity)	(spontaneous, shared recreational activity)

The initiative of seeking integration through physical education may come from a physical education specialist in a 'normal' school or from a 'special' school teacher, but either could use this basic pattern.

The *contact* stage is the initial move to seek an appropriate group with which a common experience may be shared (*involvement*). When the third stage – *interaction* phase, or the phase of optimum integration – is reached, differences are shelved and handicapped and non-handicapped pupils become directly involved with each other.

Potential contribution of physical education

How, therefore, can teachers using physical education as a medium promote the integration process in a special school, special unit or with atypical pupils in a normal class? The potential for development is nearly always there. Yet it does take effort on the part of the teacher and there may be many disappointments before satisfactory progress is made.

First, physical education and recreation provide the opportunity for the *contact* phase: physical activities always require direct involvement. Thus certain games and some forms of dance provide ready-made situations in their format or specific rules. Swimming, creative dance and gymnastics provide equal opportunities, though less formally. The activity initiates the contact, and once under way can lead to dynamic involvement in which there is more than just togetherness. In this second phase there is likely to be increased tolerance and acceptance of differences because attention is focused upon the activity. Teachers need to ensure, however, that all the children are equally involved as far as possible. Thirdly, of course sport is of almost universal interest and there is great value that attaches simply to a pupil's taking part. Thus mutually shared activity leads to *interaction* and a common understanding. Both handicapped and non-handicapped pupils then may be able to forget differences and interact on a personal level. As a consequence less adult support is needed and integration becomes less self-conscious.

It is, however, important to remember that not all pupils, handicapped or able-bodied, will react in the same way. It is also worth bearing in mind that barriers exist amongst those with different handicaps as well as between the handicapped and 'normal' people. Situations which arise must be handled sensitively and with understanding and not too much must be expected at first.

Special schools

Special schools provide a secure environment and, since there is usually a favourable staff–pupil ratio, children receive a great deal of individual attention. Unfortunately by their very nature such schools are almost inevitably isolated. It is important therefore that attempts are made to give pupils as much contact as possible with other people, outside their school.

Successful schemes have been set up involving boys and girls from the upper forms in secondary schools in teaching movement and swimming in ESN (S) schools (see also Chapter 2). Sometimes some aspect of mental handicap is included in a secondary school's general studies course. Often these older pupils gain as much benefit from the programme as the special school pupils. For handicapped pupils, of course, this is a positive way of assisting them to relate to other people. For the young helper, often in a one-to-one situation, confidence soon develops within the security of the activity. Yet it does take a degree of maturity to relate to low-functioning ESN (S), cerebral-palsied or maladjusted pupils. Girls are sometimes more successful in achieving such relationships than boys. One special advantage with young helpers is that they are not adults and do not look like teachers, and natural relationships thus develop more easily.

The adolescent helper in special schools contrasts with the retired person, parent or other adult helper. The latter have a lifetime of experience to back them and sometimes too much confidence: thus their enthusiasm may often need to be contained and channelled. Similarly, such helpers can become too achievement-oriented and want to see quick, concrete results for their efforts. The teacher therefore needs to be sensitive but also quite positive if the helpers are to be successful in integrating with the children.

While the interaction between an adolescent helper and an individual mentally handicapped pupil may be effective, an older helper may be needed to work with a small group of cerebral-palsied pupils because he probably has more insight and patience. On the other hand, young people with relatively few inhibitions may be very effective in motivating and developing movement drama or creative dance. Here the two groups may work together on equal terms. Parents and other adults can help in other ways: for example, guiding a group of pupils in a project like building and flying kites. Groups of adults could join in the games period so that the pupils have the opportunity of seeing other adults as models of behaviour and as friends. This is particularly rewarding for senior ESN (S) pupils.

When such projects are set up potential helpers can be invited to the school to watch sessions of physical education. It is important to have a follow-up discussion so the teacher can offer some insight into what he is trying to do and give suggestions to the helpers. Guidelines might be set out as follows:

1. The teacher is always in control and has over-all responsibility.
2. Helpers should consult the teacher on any 'new' activity that they want to initiate.
3. Sessions should take place at least once a week for half a term in order to get some continuity.
4. Basic safety policies must be made known and enforced.
5. The pupils must be encouraged to learn the helpers' names and talk to them. They must feel 'at home' with them.
6. The situation should be one of 'give and take', for while the helper often needs

to initiate activities he must not dominate the session. Sometimes the initiative must come from the handicapped pupil if there is to be real interaction.

Special schools: integration with regular schools

A lot depends on the distance between the special and regular school. Sessions can take place at either site, or at a mutually convenient venue such as a sports centre or adventure playground. The special school teacher must be prepared to find some resistance when he first tries to set up a relationship with a regular school, on the part of teachers, parents or children. This is understandable but can be overcome.

A sound start may be made by initiating a series of friendly sports matches between special and other schools; this is happening now in many areas. However, there needs to be discussion and agreement between the respective teachers regarding age, ability and size of the groups involved. For instance, it is better for older special-school pupils to interact with somewhat younger mainstream pupils. The type of handicap, of course, is the real determining factor. However, the difficulty with matches is that only a select few benefit from the opportunity.

On a more regular basis, a combined physical education session provides better opportunity for integration. Perhaps weekly sessions alternating between the two schools are the ideal. The teachers may take alternate sessions, one teaching and the other observing or joining in. Team teaching is perhaps a better idea, with each teacher providing his particular expertise.

A less formal arrangement could be a weekly or fortnightly lunchtime together, or Friday afternoon recreation club. Often in such situations pupils in the regular school are given the opportunity to take this as a sports option for a term. In this less formal setting the opportunity for friendships to develop is probably greater than in normal lessons. A choice of minor games such as bowls, table tennis or trampolining could have great appeal. When both schools are used, there is the advantage of using a new range of equipment. In this situation the teacher's role may be greatly reduced since most pupils may not need the security of a formally organised game.

Special and mainstream school groups may already be using a shared facility, for instance adventure playgrounds, games fields, parks, recreation centres and swimming baths. In such situations joint work can be planned in a less contrived fashion and the opportunity for true integration is greater.

Other opportunities are provided by outdoor pursuits such as aquatic activities, day hikes or trails and camping. One polytechnic runs a field camp at Anglesey as part of its teacher-training course. Several different types of school attend and share the site. The schools include a group from a regular middle school, and ESN (M) and ESN (S) schools. Student teachers organise the activity programme. Besides giving teachers contact with the pupils out of school, it also gives children from different schools and backgrounds the chance to work and play together.

Integration comes naturally in some cases. Evening activities like spontaneous football, rounders or frisbee sessions often involve pupils from all three schools. One factor acting against the integration process is the need to separate the three school groups for sleeping. For the ESN (M) group personal security dictates this whilst the ESN (S) school group usually contains several youngsters adjusting to adolescence who need close supervision. Groups are mixed for meals, however.

In competitive activities such as scavenger hunts, potted sports (i.e. miniature athletics events), archery, or tug-o-war the ESN (M) and ESN (S) pupils often prefer to be involved in parallel, as they lack the confidence to commit themselves outside their secure school group. Other problems which create barriers are relative lags in socialisation and interests. These do place limits on integration at times, especially in a short one-week period. Yet after 'lights out' many conversations are overheard which reveal an obvious interest in the other groups and degree of mutual understanding. This surely is a step towards partial integration? And then in the past there have been surprises. One such session was an impromptu 'New Faces' show organised by two students with the ESN (M) and ESN (S) schools, much to the surprise of their teachers. Pupils from both schools soon became involved in shared performances, with some pupils starring who had previously been considered shy. Or similarly a couple of the ESN (M) boys developed enough skill in archery to be able to tutor the middle-school lads.

In all such approaches the degree of interaction will vary. Very often impressions and attitudes will be evolving without any obvious outward signs. Of course type and degree of handicap are important considerations. Thus with a sight-impaired or cerebral-palsied pupil a supporting and empathetic, participating role would be appropriate for a non-handicapped pupil. In contrast, with a group of young maladjusted boys, a tolerant degree of parallel play in a shared activity would be appropriate.

Whilst the integration process evolves for each individual, the staff must be aware of certain aspects which may require sensitive manipulation. Clothes-changing facilities may be best segregated to start off with, for instance, rather than shared. This is important in the case of the physically handicapped. Similarly, competition needs to be handled with care as pupils are very astute at weighing up comparable abilities. The staff should attempt to direct the involvement more towards the activity than the competitive aspect of it. Another consideration is whether the optimum practice of mixing all the youngsters up in the teams and activities is appropriate. It may be so after a few sessions. The difficulty is not so much with the individuals as with the fact that most youngsters enjoy the identity and security of their own school group. This is true of both the handicapped and able-bodied.

In addition, teachers should highlight other aspects of the experience. The pupils can be encouraged to learn something about the other schools and to talk to one another about their experiences. At all inter-school gatherings the social side should not be forgotten; the provision of a cup of squash and biscuits can reduce embarrassment.

Special units: in school time

There is a growing trend towards incorporating 'handicapped pupils' within mainstream education by attaching a 'special unit' to a school. This enables the handicapped to have a specialist teacher and resources whilst at the same time allowing for contact with the mainstream pupils.

There is bound to be a feeling of group identity within the unit and the pupils may feel more secure working within their group. However, whenever possible they should work with other pupils; physical education is of value in promoting joint work.

Timetabling needs to be organised so that the unit pupils have all their physical education and sport sessions with the mainstream pupils. A number of schools schedule a maximum of only three handicapped children with each class. This, of course, prevents the polarisation that would occur if the whole unit attended at once.

For a physical education teacher not accustomed to handicapped pupils there are two major preliminary tasks. First, to determine the physical education needs of the unit pupils and, secondly, to decide how best to develop an integrated session. The unit class teacher can assist by first discussing individual children with the physical education teacher. A useful two-way liaison can be established by the physical education teacher's informing the unit teacher about some new area to be covered before the actual lesson. A unit session could be used then to outline, for example, a new game, theme or visit to be carried out.

The physical education teacher should know as much as possible about the special pupils, including the following:

1. Safety aspects linked with the specific handicap
2. Motor ability (i.e. endurance and flexibility)
3. The probable potential for integration
4. Needs for separate changing facilities
5. Personal hygiene (as with incontinent cases)
6. Specific teaching approaches required by the handicap
7. Realistic goals for activities and integration

With a group containing ESN (M) or (S) pupils the teacher must be conscious of the need actually to demonstrate a process rather than outline it verbally. Physically handicapped individuals may often surprise others with their success, due to determination and perseverance. Some, for instance a pupil with an osteo-condition in the gymnasium or a child with paralysed legs which scrape on the pool bottom, do need continuing special attention. Partially sighted pupils need to be informed of the layout of the apparatus in the gym or, for instance, how many steps there are between each post in a modified rounders game.

Whilst the potential for integration can only be perceived by experience in actual sessions it is useful to establish some realistic goals in advance if they are treated with some flexibility. The basic criterion for success is that the physical education sessions are still enjoyable when integrated.

Sometimes difficulties arise in situations where some allowances or modifications for unit members have to be made. Only by being positive in their teaching approach and genuine in their personal attitude can teachers make these situations acceptable to the mainstream pupils. Some handicapped children will actually resent any concessions being made and will want to stand by their own performance in the activity. Of course the teacher should consciously refrain from addressing any remarks directly to a specific group (e.g. 'the unit boys'). Another thing worth doing is to arrange the physical education roll in alphabetical order without a separate class or unit list; a minor point, but a positive contribution to the over-all effort to integrate.

While it may be appropriate to prepare the regular pupils in some classes before the first combined session this can have a discriminating effect. Some situations, however, should be discussed in advance, for instance epileptic seizures. It might be best to discuss the condition briefly during the early part of the integrated session with both unit and mainstream pupils present. It depends on the teacher's perception. Being realistic also means acknowledging that there are some limitations to what may be achieved through integration.

Some difficulties can be anticipated by the teacher, planned for and solved. But they cannot all be; for example, ESN (M) pupils often have limited concentration or motivation span in learning a skill. Even if the unit members are split up so there are only one or two in a group and the particular practice is kept interesting and short, a poor performance may not be tolerated by the regular pupils. On the other hand, in PE some ESN (M) children will be better than some of the other pupils. Different problems arise when a hearing-impaired unit is with a regular group (this is dealt with in Chapter 6). In many situations the difficulty does not lie in the specific handicap but rather in differing degrees of socialisation and maturity. A combination of contrasting activities may be one way to achieve some kind of satisfactory compromise. The opening activities could be more 'fun' oriented, yet still provide challenges for the more mature. The most successful way of achieving acceptance for children in a unit is to ensure they all have successful experiences in physical education and, where possible, on some occasions other pupils should be 'handicapped' in competitions. Some awareness of the other's situation may help increase acceptance, which is a sound start to the integration process.

Special units: out of school time

Wherever possible a child, having experienced some activities at school, should have the opportunity to experience them in a less structured environment. Principally this can be given by sports and youth clubs, sports centres, trips and camps. Thus the handicapped child can be given an experience half-way between school and open society. The unit and physical education teachers' role here would be first to liaise with the club or group leaders and secondly to make sure that the handicapped pupils are aware of the opportunities. Handicapped children often hesitate to try anything new. Their teacher may have to talk them into a trial visit or period of attendance. Once in the club or group it may be advisable for the tutor or leader to ask a mature member to pair off with a disabled youngster. There is a national network of clubs run by the Physically Handicapped and Able-Bodied Association, which has a one-to-one membership of physically handicapped and able-bodied. The main aim is to develop handicapped youngsters' ability to adapt to recreation with able-bodied people, with full integration the ultimate goal.

As members of these clubs are likely to be adolescents with their own problems of adjustment, there can be difficulties in ensuring smooth running. A realistic club leader would allow the disabled youngster to progress slowly by first just getting involved in inconspicuous activities like darts or table tennis. If he gains some degree of success in physical activity as well as pleasure and interaction with other young people, the integration process would have a sound start.

As many of these situations are likely to reflect society at large in the degree of acceptance and rebuff of the handicapped, some counselling may be appropriate. The sensitive youth leader or physical education teacher will perhaps notice difficult situations and find an opportunity to talk them over. A youngster may find he or she has no definite skill in the group or club activities. The physical education teacher at school could then give some individual coaching and time for practice.

It must be accepted that some pupils prefer the security and comradeship of a local sports club for the disabled rather than the wider range of provisions for the general public.

Regular schools: individual handicapped and atypical pupils

Because of the present emphasis upon integration and the provision of early special schooling, an increasing number of handicapped children are being educated within mainstream classes. In most schools there are other atypical pupils who must be considered to be disabled to some degree. These individuals, suffering from obesity, asthma, orthopaedic conditions, postural conditions and phobias do need support. Without encouragement physical education can exacerbate their sense of handicap.

Unfortunately, often the atypical child is excused from physical education. Teachers without experience of handicapped children often feel these children have a legitimate excuse and the often hard-pressed PE teacher does not follow up each case to see whether some participation is possible. But if he does not make an effort he is failing in his duty.

Before including such children the teacher must seek medical advice. Once medical support is given the pupil may be invited to watch for two or three weeks and notice aspects of the work he could try. The teacher may even suggest the child does not get changed at first, but just step in briefly and have a try. This could be followed by a remark like 'Right, Linda, you can do a few activities, so how about bringing some kit next week? If you get too tired you can just sit out and rest.'

During the lesson children suffering from asthma, epilepsy, arthritis, obesity or cardiac conditions must be allowed and encouraged to sit out and watch if the activity proves too much for them. Others may be able to take part in some activities but not others.

As suggested above, in some lessons temporary limitations can be placed upon the mainstream pupils in some activities. For example, the teacher can require hopping instead of running or limited possession of the ball, the creation of a dance at floor level or falling into the pool off the side instead of diving; all could help make the participation of the handicapped child more genuine for a part of the time.

Some local education authorities employ helpers especially to work with handicapped children in 'normal' schools. Most primary schools also have helpers. These often have the trust of the pupils already and can give valuable help in the PE lesson. The helper's role is often a multiple one including physical assistance, encouragement and feedback. In many instances this can contribute most of all to the ultimate integration of these individuals in the total physical education programme. The main danger is that the helper may be over-supportive and prevent the development of initiative; the teacher must be ready to step in when necessary.

The ultimate aim of all teachers and parents is that the handicapped children in their care shall be accepted as full members of society. There is certainly no easy way to bring this about, and attempts to integrate children with their peers through physical education will bring many problems. Nevertheless, this aspect of education offers excellent opportunities for 'contact', 'involvement' and 'interaction'.

Select bibliography

Specific handicaps

Anderson, E. *The Disabled School Child.* Methuen, 1973
Anderson, E. and Spain, B. *The Child with Spina Bifida.* Methuen, 1977
Committee of Enquiry. *The Education of the Visually Handicapped.* HMSO, 1972
Field, A. *The Challenge of Spina Bifida.* Heinemann Health Books, 1970
Levitt, S. *Treatment of Cerebral Palsy and Motor Delay.* Blackwell Scientific Publications, Oxford, 1977
Loring, J. *Teaching the Cerebral Palsied Child.* Spastic Society/Heinemann, 1965
Smith, V.H. and James, F.E. *Eyes and Education.* Heinemann, 1968
Spastic Society of Great Britain. *The Early Years.* London, 1967
The Hemiplegic Child. London, 1967
Facts about Cerebral Palsy. London, 1967
Wedell, K. *Learning and Perceptive Motor Disabilities in Children.* J. Wiley & Sons, 1973

Perceptual motor training

Arnheim, D.D. and Sinclair, W.A. *The Clumsy Child. A programme of Motor Therapy.* C.V. Mosby Co., St Louis, 1975
Cratty, B.J. *Motor Activity and the Education of Retardates.* Lee and Fabiger, Philadelphia, and Henry Kimpton, London, 1969
Drowatzky, J.N. *Physical Education for the Mentally Retarded.* Lee and Fabiger, Philadelphia, and Henry Kimpton, London, 1972
Frostig, M. and Maslow, P. *Movement Education: Theory and Practice.* Follett, Chicago, 1970
Morris, P.R. and Whiting, H. *Motor Impairment and Compensatory Education.* Bell & Sons, 1971

Dance and movement

Canner, N. and Klebanoff, H. *. . . And a Time to Dance.* [Relates to ESN (S)]. Beacon Press, Boston, 1968
Collins, C. *Practical Modern Educational Dance.* Macdonald & Evans, 1969
Department of Education and Science [DES]. *Movement: Physical Education in the Primary Years.* HMSO, 1972
Mason, K.C. ed. 'Dance Therapy', in *Focus on Dance*, VII. American Association of Health, Physical Education and Recreation, Washington, DC, 1973
North, M. *Movement Education.* Temple Smith, 1973

Robinson, C.M., Harrison, J., and Grindley, J. *Physical Activity in the Education of Slow-Learning Children.* [Relates to ESN (S)]. Arnold, 1970

Poetry for dance

Baldwin, F. and Whitehead, M. *That Way and This: Poetry for Creative Dance.* Chatto & Windus, 1972
Stokes, E.M. *Word Pictures as a Stimulus for Creative Dance.* Macdonald & Evans, 1970

Games and athletics

Barclay, V. *The Adaptation of Recreational Activities.* Bell & Sons, 1956
DES. *Physical Education for the Physically Handicapped.* HMSO, 1971
Disabled Living Foundation. *Sport and Physical Recreation for the Disabled.* London, 1970
Foreshaw, O. in Cooper, D. ed. *Physical Education for Handicapped Children.* PEA, 1975 (obtainable from L. Groves)
Guttman, Sir Ludwig. *Textbook of Sport for the Disabled.* H.M. and M. Publishers, 1976
'Know the Game' series, Educational Productions Ltd, Wakefield, Yorkshire [books printed in collaboration with national governing bodies of sport which give rules and basic principles]
Morgan, R.E. and Adamson, G.T. *Circuit Training.* Bell, 1961 (2nd edn)

NOTE: The Amateur Athletics Association and Women's Amateur Athletic Association of Great Britain produce their own booklets and wall charts on individual events

Adventure activities

Anderson, J.R.L. *The Ulysses Factor.* Hodder & Stoughton, 1970
Croucher, N. *Outdoor pursuits for disabled People.* Disabled Living Foundation, 1974
Cumbria LEA. 'Safety Out-of-Doors' (pamphlet; consult latest issue)
DES. *Safety in Outdoor Pursuits.* Safety Series No. 1. HMSO, 1972
Duke of Edinburgh Award Schemes Office. *Guidance for the Use of Operating Authorities in Entering and Training Physically Disabled Boys and Girls in the Duke of Edinburgh Scheme.*
Henrich and Knegel, eds. *Experiments in Survival.* Association for Aid to Crippled Children, New York, 1961
Jackson. *Special Education in England and Wales.* Oxford, 1969
National Association for Outdoor Education. 'Safety in Outdoor Education', Mar. 1972– present (consult latest issue)
Parker, T.M. and Meldrum, K.I. *Outdoor Education.* Dent, 1973
Sports Council Advisory Panel on Water Sports for the Disabled. *Water Sports for the Disabled.* Distributed by Royal Yacht Association, Seamanship Foundation (Victoria Way, Woking, Surrey), 1977

Swimming

Amateur Swimming Association. 'The Teaching of Swimming' (handbook; consult latest edition)

Elkington, H. *Swimming: A Handbook for Teachers.* Cambridge, 1978
Holmyard, T. and Elkington, H. *Better Swimming for Boys and Girls.* Kaye & Ward, 1967; repr. 1972
Newman, V.H. *Swimming and Teaching an Infant to Swim.* Angus & Robertson (UK) Ltd, 1967

Integration

Croucher, N. *Joining In: Integrated Sport and Leisure for Disabled People.* Disabled Living Foundation, Arundel, Disabilities Study Unit, 1977
Report of the Snowdon Working Party. *Integrating the Disabled.* Surrey Fine Arts Press Ltd., 1977
Warnock, M. *Special Educational Needs: Report of the Committee of Enquiry into the Education of Handicapped Children and Young People.* HMSO Command Paper 7212, 1978

Films

Produced by the Amateur Swimming Association

It's a New World 16 mm sound colour 30 mins.
Shows the potential achievements of those with differing abilities, especially in schools and clubs, and also features some of the swimmers from the Olympic Games for the Disabled
Available from: National Audio-Visual Aids Library, Paxton Place, Gypsy Rd, London SE7 9SR

Produced by the Association of Swimming Therapy

Water Free 16 mm
Shows the use of the Halliwick technique of teaching swimming and emphasises the work of the Association of Swimming Therapy
For hire and purchase from: Town & Country Productions Ltd., 21 Cheyne Row, Chelsea, London SW3 5HP

Produced by Bristol University Drama Department, with Veronica Sherborne

A Sense of Movement 16 mm sound colour 40 mins.
Veronica Sherborne's third film shows an ex-student taking movement classes with 5–8-year-old and 15–16-year-old severely retarded children. It shows how the children relate to one another and to their own bodies
Explorations 16 mm black & white 30 mins.
Shows work with the mentally handicapped
In Touch 16 mm sound black & white 30 mins.
Shows students in training and working with mentally handicapped children
All above available from: Concord Films Council, Nacton, Ipswich, Suffolk IP10 03Z

Produced by Disabled Living Foundation

Not Just a Spectator 16 mm colour 35 mins.
Shows disabled people taking part in a variety of sport and recreation including gliding, rock-climbing and caving
Available from: Town & Country Productions Ltd., 21 Cheyne Row, Chelsea, London SW3 5HP

Produced by Manchester Education Authority

I can dance 16 mm sound colour 15 mins.
Shows adolescent ESN (M) girls dancing in response to a variety of stimuli
Available from: The Visual Aids Dept, Education Offices, Crown Square, Manchester M60 3BB

Produced by the Riding for the Disabled Association

The Right to Choose 16 mm sound colour 30 mins.
Shows how horse-riding can help those with disabilities such as paraplegia, amputation and paralysis
Available from: Town & Country Productions Ltd., 21 Cheyne Row, Chelsea, London SW3 5HP

List of useful addresses

Amateur Swimming Association, Harold Fern House, Derby Square, Loughborough

Association of Swimming Therapy, c/o J. McMillan, 24 Arnos Grove, London N11

British Deaf Amateur Sports Association, 140 Green Lane, Cookridge, Leeds

British Sports Association for the Disabled, Stoke Mandeville Sports Stadium, Harvey Road, Aylesbury, Bucks. HP2 18PP

The Calvert Trust (Challenge for the Disabled) Ltd., The Calvert Trust Adventure Centre, Old Windebrowe, Keswick, Cumbria

Disabled Living Foundation, 346 Kensington High Street, London W14 8NS

Elfrida Rathbone Association, Toynbee Hall, 28 Commercial St., London E1 [Clubs for ESN (M)]

Handicapped Adventure Playground Association, 2 Paultons Street, London SW3

Institute for Research into Mental and Multiple Handicap, 16 Fitzroy Square, London W1P 5HQ

Invalid Children's Aid Association, 126 Buckingham Palace Road, London SW1 9SB

National Association for Outdoor Education, c/o Scout Dike, Outdoor Centre, Penistone, Sheffield, S30 59F

National Association of Swimming Clubs for the Handicapped, 93 The Downs, Harlow, Essex

National Council for Special Education, 1 Wood St., Stratford-on-Avon, Warwickshire, CV37 6JE

National Deaf Children's Society, 31 Gloucester Place, London NW1

National Society for Mentally Handicapped Children, 117 Golden Lane, London EC1

National Star Centre for Disabled Youth, 103 The Promenade, Cheltenham, Gloucestershire, GL50 1PE

Physical Education Association of Great Britain & Northern Ireland, Ling House, 10 Nottingham Place, London W1X 4AM

Physically Handicapped & Able-Bodied Residential and Clubs Movement (PHAB), 30 Devonshire St., London W1N 2AP

Riding for the Disabled Association, c/o Ms C. Hayes, Avenue R, National Agricultural Centre, Stoneleigh, Kenilworth, Warwickshire, CV8 2LY

Index